CONFIDENTLY COMMITTED:
A Look at the Baptist Heritage

CONFIDENTLY COMMITTED:
A Look at the Baptist Heritage

by
VIRGIL W. BOPP

Library of Congress Cataloging-in-Publication Data

Bopp, Virgil, 1927-
  Confidently committed.

  Bibliography: p.
  Includes indexes.
  1. Baptists—History. 2. Baptists—Doctrines.
I. Title.
BX6231.B67 1987   286'.09   87-23404
ISBN: 0-87227-119-6

To my mother, Mildred, who
instilled in me Christian values;

To my wife, Wilma, who
stands with me in Christ's service;

and

To my son, Bob, who
is a delight to his father's heart.

Contents

Foreword

Virgil Bopp has not written just another book on church history, but he has given us a much-needed history of those often criticized and misunderstood people—the Baptists. He qualifies well for this task, for he was reared as a child in a fundamental Baptist church, taught twenty-one years in a Baptist college (including the subjects of Baptist history and polity) and is an ordained Baptist pastor.

The author does the Christian world a great service by putting into perspective the Baptist church beginnings and development. One of the highlights of Mr. Bopp's work is the chapter entitled "The Meaning and Chronological Order of Baptist Associations." I have found that Baptists themselves do not normally understand that there are other "brands" of Baptists outside their own fellowship; therefore, it is certain that Christians in general are ignorant of the diversity among Baptists. The author makes it clear that Baptists are not some strange cult but a long-standing body of believers who essentially date back to the first century church, if not in name, certainly in practice. The author also points out that while Baptists are historically conservative Bible believers, they have many different ways of operating within the framework of the Scriptures. This diversity is reflected in the variety of church polities (government) and the strong independence displayed among individual churches.

Readers need not fear that Virgil Bopp's scholarly background will leave them wading through historical dates and jargon which the average person cannot understand. He has written to enlighten the layman as well as the student of history, and I believe you will agree that he has accomplished his task with distinction.

Jack W. Jacobs, Th.D.
Senior Pastor, Grace Baptist Church
Westlake, Ohio

Introduction

Confidently Committed was developed out of an observed need among pastors and parishioners in Baptist churches for a deeper understanding of the Baptist heritage. Reviewing the historic Baptist zeal for Bible-centered ministries is both encouraging and challenging to modern Baptists, because God's truth is unchanging and is relevant to every age and circumstance.

The purpose of *Confidently Committed* is to portray the historic Baptist movement in language understandable to a wide range of readers. In setting forth the basic Baptist tenets, we chose several representative examples from Baptist experience to validate our assertions.

No apology is given for the Biblical basis upon which the Baptist heritage rests. The Baptists of this age may give thanks for the historic Baptist positions of confidence that "the Bible taken as a whole is the only rule of faith and practice"; of personal and ecclesiastical separation and of serious and sacrificial commitment to the spread of the gospel.

I personally owe an unrepayable debt to "Bill" Kuhnle, who guided me to an understanding of being born again and making Christ Lord of my life; to Dr. R. T. Ketcham, whose faithful and dynamic pastoral teaching established in my teenage life a firm commitment to serve the Lord "whatever, whenever and wherever'' He chose; and to many relatives, parishioners, professors, colleagues and friends from whom I have learned much. With gratefulness, I also shall not forget the many students who contributed so much to my life as we gathered to learn from and about each other.

Special acknowledgement is due my family members who bore with me in this project, encouraged me and prayed with and for me. I further express my gratitude to the many friends who ministered to me as prayer partners and who shared financially, making it possible to give my undivided attention to the preparation of this manuscript.

With this material goes the hope and prayer that each reader will be challenged toward a close walk with the Lord and Savior, Jesus Christ, and led to a greater appreciation for and loyalty to the local Baptist church.

Virgil W. Bopp

1
Establishing
First Century Patterns

It is very difficult for an individual who knows the Scripture ever to get away from it. It haunts him like an old song. It follows him like the memory of his mother. It remains with him like the word of a reverenced teacher. It forms a part of the warp and woof of his life.

—Woodrow Wilson

It goes without saying that any discussion of the church must be done in the light of Scripture. In Scripture is recorded the beginning of the church. In Scripture is recorded the organizational structure of the church. In Scripture are the principles for conduct of the congregation as a whole and for individuals within the congregation. The very idea of "church" implies close attention to the statements of the Bible.

Because of this fundamental affinity, this study begins with the Biblical accounts relating to the formation of the church.

THE CHURCH DEFINED

The original New Testament used the Greek word *ekklesia*, which translated into English is *church*. Literally, the compound word (*ek-kaleo*), rearranged, means "called out ones." The New Testament as a whole teaches that the church is a people *called out of* the masses of the world population by God for the purpose of bringing glory to His name (Eph. 1:12; 3:21).

There are two uses of the word *ekklesia* in the New Testament. Of the approximately 120 times the word appears, roughly ten percent refers to a vast Universal Church made up of all true believers. Roughly ninety percent of the usages refers to local congregations of believers in clearly defined geographic areas. We will take a brief look at both usages.

THE UNIVERSAL CHURCH

The artificial term "universal," when speaking of the church, is frequently misunderstood. Some denominational groups claim this use to identify their organization as the only "true" church. Others expand it more fully to include numerous theological viewpoints under a vast ecumenical church framework.

Actually, the word "universal" is not a New Testament term. Rather, the New Testament refers to the Universal Church as the "body of Christ" (1 Cor. 12:12, 13), a "building" (1 Cor. 3:9) and a "bride" (Eph. 5:25-32; Rev. 19:7-9). An appropriate question is who or what makes up this Body of Christ, this building and this bride?

The answer is direct even though mysterious. One becomes a part of the Universal Church by being "born again" (John 3:7) and baptized into the Body by the Holy Spirit (1 Cor. 12:13). This matter of being born again needs careful Scriptural understanding. Nicodemus did not understand it at first. He even thought that Jesus meant he must return to his prenatal state and experience physical birth all over again. Jesus patiently clarified for him that one is born again of "water and of the Spirit" (John 3:5). There are many interpretations of what Jesus meant by "water." Quite obviously He did not mean simply washing the physical body with water. Paul wrote to Titus about salvation being attained by the "washing of regeneration" (Titus 3:5). Regeneration, or salvation, or being born again is through or by the Word of God (Rom. 10:17). This "Word" refers to the utterances of God as accepted or internalized, that is, made a part of the believer by faith. To construct God's method of being born again by water or Word, every individual must:

1. Recognize that he is a sinner (Rom. 3:23)
2. Realize the result of sin (Rom. 6:23)
3. Accept that God loves sinners (Rom. 5:8)
4. Acknowledge that God has provided a Savior from sin (John 3:16)
5. Become aware that he must personally accept this Savior (John 3:36)
6. Actually receive or believe in Jesus Christ as personal Savior and Lord (John 1:12; Acts 16:31)
7. Rest in the authority of God's Word as the confirmation of salvation (Titus 1:2)

The second part of Jesus' statement in John 3:5 speaks of "the spirit," or Holy Spirit. Connecting this with the Body of Christ idea, 1 Corinthians 12:13 indicates that the Holy Spirit "baptizes" the one born again into the Body of Christ, the Universal Church. In other words, the Holy Spirit is the agent Who places the individual in the Body. Theologically this is referred to as the baptism of the Holy Spirit. Although believing on the Lord Jesus Christ as personal Savior from sin and the baptism of the Holy Spirit are two distinct things, they are so intertwined as to be perceived as one simultaneous occurrence.

We will go into more detail about the Universal Church later. For now, let us suggest the following definition: The Universal Church, the Body of Christ, is comprised of all true believers from the Day of Pentecost to the rapture of the Church at the end of this age. At this present moment the Body is not fully formed, the building is not complete nor the bride fully and properly attired.

THE LOCAL CHURCH

This aspect of the word "church" is much easier to understand because it is tangible, visible and can be experienced. The local church is the working unit for gospel outreach, the primary institution through which the work of God on earth is to be carried on in this age. While the Universal Church is not an organized working unit, the local church is an organization for action. A local church is not a worldwide religious system under some hierarchy of administration. Neither is it a conglomerate body of mixed convictions. Simply stated, a local church is a body of baptized (immersed) believers of like faith in a given locality, banded together for the purpose of orderly carrying forth the gospel, fulfilling the ordinances, dependent only upon God for its leadership and organization (Acts 2:41; 20:28; 1 Cor. 3:16; 12:27; Eph. 2:20, 21; 1 Tim. 3:15).

The organization of the local church is briefly summarized in Philippians 1:1, "Paul and Timotheus, the servants of Jesus Christ, to all the *saints* in Christ Jesus which are at Philippi, with the *bishops* and *deacons*." The verse indicates a body of believers with some leaders called bishops and deacons. The bishops were the basic overseers of the local church and the deacons cared for the more temporal matters. In the New Testament there is no provision for a pastoral dictator or spiritual superior. Instead, the idea of leadership is tied up with loving service. This made the local church a community of believers, people with similar beliefs and practices, who were dedicated to serving each other, edifying and encouraging each other, discipling and disciplining each other and spreading the good news of salvation to their immediate environment and on to the ends of the earth.

Although there is no direct command in Scripture for membership in a local church, the command is implied. First and 2 Corinthians show a definite decision being made about a moral problem, and Paul indicates that they should put the erring one out of the membership (1 Cor. 5:13, Williams translation). Acts 2 also suggests that those who believed and were baptized were added to the church, and since this account took place in the city of Jerusalem, the verse must be referring to a local church. Membership symbolizes being a part of the Universal Church and, therefore, is attained on the basis of personally being born again and being baptized as a testimony of identification with the Savior.

In Acts 6, some of the members or constituents were being neglected. The fellowship had literally mushroomed and the apostles were not able to care for all the work. Seeing this need, the apostles suggested to the church that they choose some spiritual men from among them to assist in the work of the church. The people then chose seven men "of honest report, and full of the Holy Ghost" to serve in a special ministering capacity. The Greek word *diakonia* is used here and comes over into English as *deacon*. These deacons had a specific responsibility of caring for the widows and other needy ones.

It is interesting to note that the apostles were concerned with their time for study of the Word and spiritual leadership. One would think that the apostles who had been with Jesus would have had an extremely superior position, but they did not apparently see themselves that way. In spiritual humility, these men were led of the Holy Spirit to use the Greek word *diakonia*, a servant, to describe their role of sharing the Word with the people.

With these brief insights into a New Testament description of a local church, we see that Paul had some genuine, spiritual understanding when he admonished that people in churches were to love and "serve one another" (Gal. 5:13), "submit to one another" (Eph. 5:21) and esteem each other better than themselves (Phil. 2:3). What an example for future generations to follow!

These people, banded together in loving fellowship, had a very important mission. Essentially they were to carry out the Great Commission of Matthew 28:19 and 20. To accomplish this there was a five-fold breakdown of tasks:

1. Preach the Word (1 Cor. 1:21)—evangelism
2. Teach the Word (2 Tim. 2:2)—edification
3. Carry the Word (Acts 20:20)—visitation
4. Study the Word (2 Tim. 2:15)—literature
5. Send the Word (Acts 13:3)—missions

With dedication, ambition and spiritual enthusiasm the fledgling churches carved a path through the spiritual wilderness of the first century world. There were no precedents, no past experiences. These believers could only depend upon the words of the Savior while He was here on earth and the work of the Holy Spirit upon the minds and lives of holy men and women.

THE CHURCHES IN ACTION
IN THE FIRST CENTURY

The account of the churches in action begins with the coming of Jesus Christ. Numerous prophetic statements in the Old Testament pointed to a coming Messiah. These prophetic words described the place, the family line and many of the circumstances that would characterize His coming into the world. Careful study of the Scripture reveals that each of these Old Testament types, pictures and promises were fulfilled in Jesus of Nazareth.

Virgin born of Mary, Jesus grew and matured physically as normal people do. But there was something extraordinary about Him. At the age of twelve, for instance, He is found in a temple discussing things with the priests. The priests were amazed. His parents, who thought perhaps He was with relatives, returned to discover Him in this significant discussion. They began to chastise Him—but Jesus reminded them of the importance of doing His Father's business (Luke 2:49). At the time, Joseph and Mary failed to comprehend His meaning.

John the Baptist, six months older than Jesus, set a unique stage for the coming ministry of Jesus. He preached repentance from sin and conducted water baptism which pointed forward to the Savior to come (Acts 19:1-5). One day as this strangely dressed man of the desert was preaching to a curious crowd, Jesus came by. John paused, pointed to Jesus and described Him as the Lamb of God Whose purpose was to take away the sin of the world (John 1:29). Later, Jesus was baptized by John as a living example of obedience, and His earthly ministry was begun.

As we reflect on the church, one of the key events in the ministry of Jesus was an encounter He had with Peter in Matthew 16. Peter had responded correctly in identifying Jesus as the "Christ, the Son of the living God." The Master Teacher rewarded Peter for his correct answer by challenging him to understand something far reaching. Christ depicted Peter as a little stone and then stated that He would build His church on a great rock. Whether or not Peter understood the full meaning at that moment, he did clearly see it when penning under inspiration the words of 1 Peter 2:4-9. The foundation upon which the church was to be built was Jesus Christ Himself. Paul supports this truth in 1 Corinthians 3, pointing out that other foundations are erroneous and, like building a house on the sand, the superstructure falls at the slightest challenge (Matt. 7:26, 27; Luke 6:49).

The teachings of Jesus were met with mixed responses. The common people listened attentively because His message lightened some of the restrictive, petty, burdensome rules of the Pharisees. He made religion simple and sensible. But His teachings were not easy to observe. For example, He taught people the necessity of forgiving those who harmed them and even told them to love their enemies. Over and over again, Jesus illustrated His teachings by healing diseases, restoring the incapacitated to normal functioning, casting out demons, feeding the hungry and forgiving sins. Thrilled with His teaching and example, some people wanted to make Him a king right away.

However, not everyone listened to Jesus with gladness. Many rich people hated Him because He interfered with their selling of animals for temple sacrifices at a great profit. Some of the rebellious common people hated Him because He refused to use His power to drive out the Roman overlords who held them in bondage. The Pharisees hated Him because they were creators of numerous extraneous rules, and Jesus broke some of their rules.

Out of this vast milieu Jesus called, or chose, disciples whom He named "Fishers of men." To these inner-circle men and a few others He gave special responsibility for the furtherance of God's gospel. Some of these struggled, one utterly failed, and by the time of the crucifixion most of them were following at a distance. He had given instruction, however, that soon after His return to the Father in Heaven His faithful, believing followers would receive the Holy Spirit and thereby be given strength to witness to the world. After Christ's resurrection and ascension, 120 men and women were gathered in a meeting place. There had been rumors about the impossibility of His resurrection. Soldiers had been posted to guard against stealing the body. Although skeptics abounded, these

120 had talked with the risen Lord and now fifty days after the crucifixion, ten days after the ascension, they waited and were rewarded.

Pentecost—a sound of rushing wind filled the room. What appeared to be a flame of fire lighted upon each one. Immediately they began to talk in numerous intelligible languages. Word spread. Crowds gathered out of curiosity. Some inquisitors were amazed, others thought the disciples were intoxicated, but everyone heard the gospel message in his own language. Filled with and led by the Holy Spirit, Peter addressed the crowd, declaring that Jesus had died, risen again and ascended back into Heaven. He had come to save men and women, and now each one must receive Him by faith as personal Savior and be baptized in water as a testimony of identification to all the world. On that memorable day three thousand believed, were baptized and were added to the number of disciples. *The church was born.* These believers became active in spreading the truth of God's salvation, they met daily for fellowship and gladness filled their hearts. ". . . And the Lord added to the *church* daily such as should be saved" (Acts 2:47).

From Pentecost to the present, the history of the church is that men and women touched others with the gospel of God's grace unto salvation. Only a few names are recorded, but many were involved. The book of Acts and the Epistles explain in some detail the wildfire spread of the church in those early years. A worldwide period of peace was in effect. The ungodly Roman rule was being used by God for the spread of the gospel. There were no wars—the Roman legions saw to that. There were adequate roads—the Roman military engineers saw to that. There was freedom to travel without passport, visa or customs because all the known world was governed by Rome. Certainly Paul's words in Galatians 4:4, "When the fulness of the time was come, God . . ." were true. Never before and not since that time has the world been in such a conducive state for the introduction of something new—and God used that moment to bring into the world His institution, the church.

During these apostolic years, letters were written and made a part of Holy Scripture. "Holy men of God" wrote as the Holy Spirit moved them (2 Pet. 1:21) and a set of principles for the churches was forged and hammered out on the anvil of God's time. These writings stood the test of time and became the instruction material for local church operation in that first century A.D. All around the Mediterranean area churches were begun, and other histories show churches being founded in Armenia, Parthia, Persia, Assyria, India, Egypt and many other places. In a definite sense the pattern of Acts 1:8 was carried out: "But ye shall receive power, after that the Holy Ghost is come upon you: and ye shall be witnesses unto me both in Jerusalem, and in all Judea, and in Samaria, and unto the uttermost part of the earth."

When the apostles died, other leaders rose to take their places. History calls them Church Fathers. They were pastors (or as they were then called, bishops) who were highly esteemed by their loyal local congregations and were especially looked up to by others for leadership. The word "Father" was used of these men out of a sense of esteem, not because they were ancestral. History refers to the immediate successors of the apostles who lived during Jesus' time as Apostolic Fathers. These Apostolic Fathers were one generation removed from the founding of the church and faced different experiences.

While the apostle John (the last of the apostles to pass from the scene) was writing the book of the Revelation while exiled on the island of Patmos, the pastor (bishop) at Rome was a man named Clement. The church at Corinth asked him for assistance in putting down a disturbance there. He sent a letter encouraging them to demonstrate Christian graces in their daily relationships to one another and to their pastors and deacons. His writings, though extra-Biblical, are given a place in refining the activities of the church.

A few years later, Ignatius, pastor (bishop) at Antioch in Syria, was arrested and sent to Rome for execution for his Christian faith. He wrote seven letters on the way to Rome which stressed the need for unity. This unity was to be accomplished by rooting out heresies that denied the full divine-human personality of Christ and that preached subjection of all local church leaders to a ruling bishop. Already the oneness of the believers in local churches was being subverted. The democratic system was giving way to a hierarchical system.

There were many other Apostolic Fathers, but Polycarp, pastor at Smyrna (located in what is now Turkey) will be the last in this discussion. He was a disciple of the apostle John and wrote a letter to the Philippians emphasizing the need to exercise faith in Christ and the need to let that faith be worked out in daily living.

The end of the first century found the theology of the Apostolic Era substantially firm. First, Jesus was the Mediator of the New Covenant, the church in the New Testament. Second, the Word of God (the Old and New Testament writings themselves) was authoritative. Third, the ordinances (they referred to them as sacraments) of baptism and the Lord's Supper were to be observed. And fourth, each believer was a spiritual priest with direct access to God. In the next few hundred years after the era of the Apostolic Fathers, great changes came about in the organized churches: the church hierarchy became the earthly mediator of religious matters; tradition was given equal force with Scripture; the sacraments were expanded from two to seven and made to be a means of attaining grace unto salvation, and a professional priesthood began to intercede for the people of the faith.

The era of the Apostolic Fathers is a portrait of a church with a vibrant missionary zeal, a church which recognized individual responsibility and a church with a minimum of organization. However, seeds were being sown for the future by emphasizing baptism, martyrdom and celibacy as having some special sin-atoning power.

Many accepted these "small changes" without question. Others sought to preserve local churches in simplicity. In the years to follow (A.D. 100 to 1500), the human element was intertwined with the divine element in the churches so that only a few held any close resemblance to the church of the New Testament.

2
Baptist Uniqueness

O Word of God incarnate,
O Wisdom from on high,
O Truth unchanged, unchanging,
O Light of our dark sky;
We praise Thee for the radiance
That from the hallowed page,
A lantern to our footsteps,
Shines on from age to age.

O make Thy church, dear Savior,
A lamp of purest gold,
To bear before the nations
Thy true light, as of old.
O teach Thy wandering pilgrims
By this their path to trace,
Till clouds and darkness ended,
We see Thee face to face!
                                    —William W. How

The many denominational groups that have divided the world of Christendom are differentiated from one another by a belief or practice that makes each group unique. There has been a tendency to minimize these differences since the interdenominational and nondenominational movements of the first half of the twentieth century. With the rise of massive organizations came a further mingling of ideas and a call for unity through what is called the ecumenical movement. The objectives of ecumenism include emphasizing similarities, promoting consensus and agreeing to work together in unity without total conformity in belief. One of the results of ecumenism has been a confusion of beliefs and standards so that churches are not clearly identified as to theology or practice. This has been true of nearly all major denominational groups in some way.

In the early part of the twentieth century there was a clear division between modernism and fundamentalism on a theological base. Fundamentalism was a very unique movement, separated from almost all mainline denominations. Few people wished to adopt that "fundamentalist" identification because it seemed extremely restrictive. By the beginning of the 1980s, the fundamentalist name had lost some of its "punch" and many groups accepted the name gladly. The media also called significant attention to it. It seems that the tendency is always away from uniqueness and toward commonality, or as some would suggest, toward compromise.

Baptist groups are not exempt from such tendencies. In order to gain acceptance and strength, many of them have drifted away from the historic Baptist system of faith and practice, or the "Baptist Distinctives." Applying this uniqueness statement makes it possible to analyze current Baptist groups as to their closeness to the historic position.

There are many ways to express this position. Some have chosen to use an acrostic:

> B—Biblical authority
> A—Autonomy of the local church
> P—Priesthood of the believer
> T—Two church officers
> I—Individual soul liberty
> S—Saved church membership
> T—Two church ordinances
> S—Separation of church and state

Other groups stretch these distinctives into nine or ten

statements, while still others combine some so that they have only five or six. It is true that many denominational groups accept some of these statements whole-heartedly, but historic Baptists are the only ones who accept the complete list. Even some groups who call themselves Baptist no longer hold to these historic principles. For our purposes here, we will use a combination of the above principles.

First, Baptists have historically held that *the Bible taken as a whole is the only rule for faith and practice*. Every Baptist statement of faith or written confession—such as the Philadelphia, New Hampshire and Baptist Bible Union—begins with this fundamental of fundamentals. The Philadelphia Confession of Faith opens with: "The Holy Scripture is the only sufficient, certain, and infallible rule of all saving knowledge, faith and obedience. . . ." An examination of other Protestant confessions indicates the absence of this clear statement. The Westminster Confession, for instance, states in effect that although nature and creation are enough to render man inexcusable before God, it pleased God to provide man with a written record. This approach of "playing down" the importance of the Bible is even reflected in architecture. Many churches have a divided pulpit with an altar in the central place. Historic Baptist churches have the pulpit from which the Bible is expounded in the central place, emphasizing the significance of Scripture in church and personal life.

Many Baptist preachers of the nineteenth century used a certain motto to reflect the importance of the Bible: "Where the Scriptures speak, we speak; where they are silent, we are silent." Because of this approach, the preachers were great defenders of the faith without expending great time and energy on peripheral issues or extra-Biblical disputes. To historic Baptists the preaching of the Bible was the most important thing because (1) it was the only means by which any person could become a Christian, and (2) believers needed to know the Bible well in order to participate in the decision-making process of congregational government in their local churches.

J. M. Cramp in his *Baptist History* said, "The distinguishing principle of the Baptists was clearly discerned by our British forefathers, and consistently maintained. They owned no master but Christ, no rule but His Word."[1] J. B. Edmonson in *What Baptists Stand For* says, "With us, nonessentials are the opinions of the Fathers and the things received by tradition. The essentials are the things that Christ has commanded."[2]

It is one thing to believe that the Bible is the only rule of faith and practice; it is another to believe that the Bible *taken as a whole* is the only rule of faith and practice. Baptists have historically held that the entirety of Scripture (the sixty-six books of the Old and New Testaments) is inspired of God, and that whatever comes from God is perfect and has no mixture of error. Many people develop a basic belief system from a small, isolated portion of Scripture. To avoid misinterpretation, Baptists have insisted that no passage stands alone, but that every passage is interpreted by the rest of Scripture.

Upon this basic belief of the authority of Scripture taken as a whole (2 Tim. 3:16, 17; 2 Pet. 1:19-21), Baptists have constructed each of their distinctive positions. Exiled from his homeland, threatened by circumstances and wondering if he would ever come to his inherited throne, David asked, "If the foundations be destroyed, what can the righteous do?" (Ps. 11:3). One interpretation of this passage is that the Bible must be the foundation of faith and practice, and if this foundation is removed for any reason, the believer becomes unstable, and church principles and practices are open to every human pronouncement. The basic principle of Biblical authority is the fundamental support for historic Baptists.

The second distinguishing mark of historic Baptists is that *only those who are genuinely saved through faith in Jesus Christ, and can give a worthy testimony thereof, can be a member of a Baptist church*. One of the requirements for membership in a historic Baptist church was a significant verbal testimony of the individual's recognition of sinfulness and belief in Jesus Christ as personal sin-bearer. There was no hint of what is called "easy believism" in the historic Baptist churches. When a person was saved, it

---

1. J. M. Cramp, *Baptist History* (London: Elliot Stock, 1868), 362.
2. From J. Irving Reese, *A Guide for Organizing and Conducting a Baptist Church* (Hayward, CA: J. F. May Press, 1952), 11.

was more than just an escape from hell; it was a salvation for living day by day. Historic Baptists noted that salvation came by believing on the Lord Jesus Christ (Acts 16:31), which meant that the believer recognized a divine control over his actions in his everyday affairs.

Historic Baptists insisted that believing came first, followed by baptism and church membership. This was a very different response to the Scriptures than given by most Protestant groups. Historic Baptists rejected the idea of infant baptism because there was no way for the child to be saved or to believe on his own behalf. They also rejected the idea of salvation by proxy, which meant that parents could believe for their children, because again the child was not believing on his own behalf.

As further evidence of personal salvation, Baptists expected to see proof of repentance (a changed attitude toward sin) and proof of conversion (an actual turning away from sin). James 2:17 was interpreted literally, "Even so faith, if it hath not works, is dead, being alone." Every person is saved for himself and furthermore must serve and obey the Savior for himself. Christ chose individuals for the purpose of bearing fruit (Gal. 5:22-26), and therein is God the Father glorified (John 15:8). Dr. Howard Fulton, addressing the assembled Regular Baptist delegates in 1932 said: "An apple tree is not an apple tree because it bears apples, but an apple tree bears apples because it is an apple tree. Fruit is the result of life, not the cause of it. Christian works are the evidence of Christian life."

All members of historic Baptist churches were to be born of God by His Word (John 3:5; James 1:18; 1 Pet. 1:23) and obedient to the commands of the Savior as found in the Scriptures. One of the practical methods used to satisfy this requirement was a personal testimony to those already in the local membership. Since the existing membership and the applicant were human, it was possible that some could know the language but not have the actual heart experience of salvation, thereby being able to fool the hearers. In case of a false testimony, Baptists looked for the evidence of a changed life and sometimes even allowed a period of time between salvation and church membership to observe the applicant's behavior and life-style. Although no amount of human requirements is foolproof, it has been important to Baptists to be as careful as possible in not allowing nonbelievers into church membership.

The third distinguishing characteristic of Baptists is that *believer's immersion is the only Biblical form of baptism.* Scriptural proof is found in the commandment of Christ in Matthew 28:19 and 20 and in the practice and teaching of the churches as seen in Acts 8:36-39, Romans 6:1-18 and Colossians 2:12. In each instance the believing came before the immersion.

Immersion is also proven to be the Scriptural mode of baptism on the basis of a more literal translation from the Greek to English. The Greek word *baptizo* literally means "to dip." It was used in classical Greek to refer to a ship which for some reason had been submerged and was subsequently raised from the water again. For the Baptists, there was no room for the acceptance of sprinkling or pouring as a mode for baptism. Although many suggest that the King James text of 1611 has a better authenticity than most other translations, its treatment of *baptizo* has caused great confusion. A study of church history reveals that by the seventeenth century, the Roman church had fully accepted sprinkling as a form of baptism. The large baptistries in Roman cathedrals of southern Europe are testimony of earlier baptism by immersion by priests, bishops and even popes. When the Anglican church (the Church of England) was formed in protest to foreign influence by the Roman church, they continued the practice of baptism by sprinkling. King James was the head of both state and church. He authorized the translation of the Bible into English from some very early manuscripts. The translators, perhaps not willing to offend the king, came to *baptizo* and instead of translating, transliterated the word into *baptism.* This opened the way for confusion that exists to this present day.

Furthermore, Baptists see immersion as an appropriate symbol of some spiritual events. One, it is a picture of the believer's identification with the death, burial and resurrection of Christ. When Christ died, the believer died. When Christ was buried, the believer was buried. When Christ rose from the grave, the believer rose from the grave. This is a transaction of faith, of course, not an actual occurrence. Two, it is a picture of the believer's death to the *old man* and resurrection to the *new man*. In 2 Corinthians 5:17, Paul talks of a "new creature," and in Romans 6, Ephesians 4 and Colossians 3 he refers to putting off an "old man" and putting on a "new man." Three, it is a prophetic picture of the future resurrection of the believer's body from the grave (1 Cor. 15:51-58).

In some descriptions of Baptist uniqueness, the second of the church ordinances, the Lord's Supper (or communion), is thoroughly discussed at this point. A brief statement will be sufficient here. Baptists have held that those who participate in the communion service should be obedient Christians. The ordinance has no saving merit but does indicate the fulfilling of a command of Christ and Paul (Luke 22; 1 Cor. 11). The individual believer is to examine *himself* prior to participating. The elements, broken unleavened bread and the fruit of the vine, are symbolic of Christ's broken body and shed blood. Baptists, therefore, reject the beliefs of transubstantiation and consubstantiation. For Baptists, this ordinance belongs to the custody of the local church for its administration. Generally, they have insisted that to participate in this service the individual should determine his own relationship with God:

1. Have I believed on the Lord Jesus Christ as my personal Savior?
2. Have I been baptized by immersion in obedience to His commands?
3. Have I become a participating member of a local church?
4. Is there anything hindering my relationship with God that needs to be made right? And if so, have I made it right?

Some Baptists practice open communion, leaving the decision to participate up to the individual. Other Baptists practice closed communion, making membership in the local church where the service is being held a prerequisite for partaking of the elements.

The fourth mark of Baptist uniqueness is belief in the *sovereignty of the local church*. Any statement of this nature assumes some type of proper organization for the local church. This organization consists of a pastor (pastors), a board of deacons and the congregation. A local Baptist church may, within Biblical limits, organize itself in nearly any way it wishes. Thus, Baptist churches have many other officers—they are deemed necessary by the congregation to carry out the functions of the church in an orderly fashion. Sovereignty simply means that a duly organized local church owns and controls itself. Each local Baptist church is an independent unit, responsible to no one but Jesus Christ, the Head of the church, transacting its own business, ordaining and instituting its own programs, determining its own voluntary course of cooperation and fellowship with other churches and organizations, and deferring to no higher earthly court of appeals than itself.

Two prominent words add to a further description of local church sovereignty. *Indigenous* means that the local church naturally belongs and grows in a certain geographic location. Indigenous also means that each local church reflects its own environment. A person traveling around the world will notice that local Baptist churches have individuality in architecture, style of service and manner of bearing. The indigenous part of church sovereignty allows for individual characteristics without demanding conformity to any design, liturgy or conduct. Interpreting the Scriptures for itself, each local church has a unique character and personality.

The second important word to help define sovereignty is *autonomous*. Basically, this word deals with independence from outside influence and financial support. Local Baptist churches historically stand separate from outside ecclesiastical authority whether it be an association, convention, conference or bureaucratic hierarchy. Furthermore, Baptist churches have withstood interference from political institutions and legislative power in conducting their internal affairs.

Because the sovereign local Baptist church owns and controls itself, it has several Biblical responsibilities:

1. Determining its own membership (1 Tim. 5:9)
2. Determining its own offices (Phil. 1:1)
3. Choosing its own officers (Acts 6:1-6)
4. Establishing its own standards for members and disciplining them for failure to live up to them (1 Cor. 5:13)

5. Celebrating the ordinances (Acts 2:41, 42; 1 Cor. 11:23-26)
6. Determining its own system of finance (1 Cor. 16:1-3)
7. Establishing its own system or style of worship and service outreach (1 Cor. 14:40; Col. 2:5)
8. Settling its own internal affairs (1 Cor. 6:1-5)
9. Determining its own relationships with other churches and organizations (Acts 15:1-30)
10. Owning property and determining how it shall be used (Acts 2:44, 45)
11. Defending its right to self-government (Matt. 18:15-17)
12. Expecting proper respect for church leaders (Heb. 13:17; 1 Pet. 5:2)

The local Baptist church exists for the purpose of obediently carrying out the commands of Christ, Who is exalted to the preeminent place as each member seeks to know and do the will of God as revealed in His Word. Baptists, therefore, must be people of the Bible. If a local church is to operate (as it declares) in a congregational form, it requires knowledgeable church members. Each must know his Bible well. In Baptist history this is referred to as the Freedom Principle, meaning that each member is free to participate in the decision-making process of his sovereign local church. Baptists have always been concerned with a teaching-evangelistic preaching ministry, participation in the Sunday School movement from its inception, active involvement in the academy (Christian elementary school) movement and establishment of many schools to provide Biblically and practically prepared ministers and missionaries. Carefully prepared leaders carefully prepare their people to make careful decisions in the local church and in their respective personal lives.

The fifth distinguishing feature of historic Baptists is probably the most unique and maligned characteristic—*the soul liberty of the individual believer*. Most denominations exert a rather significant system of control over their members. It should be understood that certain controls are necessary for people to live harmoniously together, but for Baptists these controls are tied in with the priesthood of every believer. Baptists have consistently taught that every believer has direct access to God, the only mediator being Jesus Christ, the Great High Priest (Heb. 5:1-10; 1 Pet. 2:5-9; Rev. 1:5, 6; 5:10; 20:6).

After approximately 1950, a call for freedom to "do your own thing" became a strong influence upon the Western world. Young people rejected restrictions of all kinds. The violence of the 1960s was a demonstration of a generation out of control. Every traditional social institution—government, family, education, religion and economics—was questioned and generally rejected. This attitude challenged the traditional churches and especially the Baptist concept of "soul liberty." Liberty had become license!

Soul liberty for the historic Baptist has never been a license to violate any command of God, any law of the land, any family affinity, any study of mind and character building material or any system requiring a man to be worthy of payment for a task. Instead, soul liberty asks the individual believer-priest to act in a conscionable manner, accepting the responsibility for his actions. Soul liberty involves individual freedom under the Lordship of Christ (Matt. 23:8; Rom. 10:9, 10). The individual is responsible to God, with the aid of his church, to live as a good steward of all God has given him, because one day he will have to give account of himself to God (Rom. 14:12).

This kind of restrictiveness is not in the spirit of legalism, with which much of evangelicalism and fundamentalism countered the "freedom" of the 1950s and 1960s. Neither is it rooted in the permissiveness that other social and religious groups used in a switch to the "new morality." While no one on earth has the power to control another person's soul liberty, it becomes restricted by the Holy Spirit, Who takes the Word of God and plants it deeply in the mind and life of each believer, so behavior is rationally and spiritually carried out.

Soul liberty meant to the historic Baptist believer that he had been persuaded to live in Biblical, moral patterns based upon Scripture. The church's responsibility is not to threaten, cajole or dictate but to so clearly present the Scriptures in the power of the Holy Spirit as to convince individuals to do right (Rom. 4:21; 2 Cor. 5:11). The persuaded person then develops a sanctified conscience because it has been brought under the control of the Lordship of Jesus Christ (Acts 23:1; 24:16).

Logically, it follows that the person's motivation is changed (Titus 1:12-16). This freedom into which the believer comes gives him a "want to" not a "have to" motivation. Paul told Titus (Titus 3:8) that those who believe in God should do good works because they are "good and profitable unto men." Baptist churches have a grave responsibility to teach and instruct their members in the Word—this is a divine trust (2 Tim. 4:1, 2).

The believer-priest, acting out his soul liberty, must know Bible content, doctrine and principles. This kind of liberty takes into consideration the believer's own person and body, the effect on other believers, the effect on nonbelievers and the effect on the name of Jesus when a particular life-style is chosen and acted out. In this way the believer's mind and the mind of God coincide in genuine harmony.

The sixth and last of the characteristics which make Baptists different from other groups is their historic stance on the *separation of church and state*. The church as an organization is not to interfere with the functioning of the state, and neither is the state to interfere with the functioning of the church. They are to be separate from each other because they serve in different spheres.

God established the institution of the state, or human government, immediately following the great flood of Noah's time (Gen. 8; 9). In God's view, the state exists for the purpose of keeping people from destroying each other. The state is the institution charged to keep order in the society—protecting life, property and individual freedoms or rights. The state's functioning is in the area called temporal. Matthew 22:21 sharply and clearly defines limitations: ". . . Render . . . unto Caesar the things which are Caesar's; and unto God the things that are God's." The state is not to invade the religious sphere of things eternal.

The responsibilities of the church as an institution are to preach the gospel, observe the ordinances and care for its membership spiritually and in the time of material need. The church is as limited by Matthew 22:21 as is the state. The church is not to participate in political activity but is to limit itself to spiritual pursuits. The apostles did not try to remedy societal problems through church action, but they did produce good men whose lives were a positive influence on their world. It is important to note that Biblical Christianity in the form of local churches has existed in places where the political arenas were very different. Vibrant churches existed under Roman political pressure and persecution, during the days called the "Dark Ages" and during the ages of despotic kings who believed themselves nearly omnipotent. Aggressive churches existed in the early days of opening doors to carry the gospel to the ends of the earth. They thrived under the democratic state principle as it expanded over the Western world, and they thrive today in the parts of the world where totalitarian, atheistic Communism oppresses them on every hand. The local churches, sovereign as they may be, are hard to destroy. It seems that when oppression or persecution delivers a crushing blow to one local church, at least one other church springs up somewhere else.

The state and the church are capable of four different relationships. The church may be under the state, as in nations where a state-run church exists and in Communist countries. The state may be under the church, as was true in the medieval world and most of the Spanish conquered Western world. The church may be alongside the state in a cooperative way, as in most of the Scandinavian countries. Or, the state and the church may be utterly free from each other—a free state which allows no substitution for the free exercise of religion.

The task of the church is pictured for us in the Old Testament. God gave to the world judges to straighten out all the ills of the Hebrew society. One after another they sought to alleviate the corruption, immorality and sinfulness of their world. Each in turn failed. Confusion reigned. But note the first verse of the book of Ruth: "Now it came to pass in the days when the judges ruled. . . ." Right in the middle of all the confusion and strife, God gives a love story. The great mission of the local Baptist churches is to tell the love story of Jesus Christ's love for mankind, and His desire for men and women to love Him in return in every kind of situation.

Historic Baptists have held to the free church and free state idea because of a Biblical base (Matt. 22:21; Rom. 13:1-7; Heb. 13:7, 17).

Civil governments, rulers and magistrates are to be respected, and in all temporal matters, not contrary to conscience and the word of God, to be obeyed: but they have no jurisdiction in spiritual concerns, and have no right of dictation to, or control over, or of interference with, matters of religion; but are bound to protect all good citizens in the peaceable enjoyment of their religious rights and privileges.

No organic union of Church and State should be tolerated, but entire separation maintained: the Church should neither ask for, nor accept of, support from civil authority, since to do so would imply the right of the civil dictation and control. The support of religion belongs to those who profess it.

Christian men are to be good and law-abiding citizens, sustaining and defending the government under which they live, in all things not contrary to conscience and the word of God; while such government is bound to protect them in the full enjoyment of all their rights and privileges, both civil and religious.[3]

The Pilgrim Fathers came to Plymouth with the great desire for a free church in a free state. The writings of John Robinson, William Bradford and William Brewster clearly establish their moralistic approach to these freedoms. The Puritans, on the other hand, took a much more legalistic stance in government influence on religion. It is interesting to note that when Roger Williams (the generally accepted founder of the Baptist movement in America) came declaring that "the civil magistrate's power extends only to the bodies and goods and outward state of man,"[4] he was banished by the Puritans but was gladly received by the Pilgrims and accepted by many of the Indians.

An illustration from Rhode Island reflects the Baptist view on separation of church and state. One day, the citizens of

3. Edward T. Hiscox, *The New Directory for Baptist Churches*, propositions VII, VIII and IX (Philadelphia: Judson Press, 1953), 12-13.
4. Theodore P. Greene, ed., *Roger Williams and the Massachusetts Magistrates* (Boston: D.C. Heath and Company, 1964), 4.

Providence began taking steps to organize a militia. A number of citizens objected because of religious scruples. Roger Williams responded by giving his famous simile: "A ship is at sea. It is like a civil commonwealth. On board are Roman Catholics, Protestants, Jews and Moslems. None should be compelled to attend the ship's worship, or be prevented from their own particular worship, if any. But the captain should command the course of the ship, and none may refuse to do what is required for the common safety."[5]

Historic Baptists have a uniqueness in belief and practice. They have emphatically insisted on:

1. The absolute authority of the Bible taken as a whole as the only rule for faith and practice
2. A church membership made up of only those who give a worthy testimony to a genuine saving faith through the Lord Jesus Christ
3. Immersion as the only Biblical form of baptism
4. The sovereignty of each local church in caring for its internal affairs and external affiliations
5. The absolute soul liberty of the individual believer-priest as he lives out his life under the Lordship of Jesus Christ
6. The separation of church and state, allowing freedom for the state in temporal matters and freedom for the church in things spiritual and eternal

Many religious groups subscribe to some of these distinctives, but most do not accept them all. Even some Baptist bodies have either rejected some or perhaps agreed to them with tongue in cheek. At the very least, each Baptist church has a responsibility to examine itself in the light of this distinctive heritage.

5. Reprinted from the April 1954 issue of the *Crusader* upon resolution of the General Council of the American Baptist Convention.

3
The Question of Baptist Origins

What the Baptists stand for was set in motion by God Himself—and surely there is no end to that, not only to the story (of Baptists) but to the eternal fact itself. As long as the surf pounds the ocean shores, as long as trees and grasslands turn green in the springtime these ideas and the work that goes with them will point to ever new beginnings in life.

—R. Dean Goodwin

The quest for knowledge regarding the people, denominational organization and belief system called Baptist requires a look at the very earliest examples of those holding the Baptist Distinctives. Each and every religious movement comes from some historical antecedent. In an entirely different context than this present discussion, James Baldwin wrote, in effect, "We cannot escape our origins, however hard we try." Many speak disparagingly of Baptists because they do not understand the background, the cost and the dedicated effort that brought this movement to its present hour. Knowledge of the heritage of any group will often lead to deeper understanding and tolerance. Even where men vehemently disagree there can be respect for each one's human dignity and worth.

Origin means parentage, ancestry or derivation and implies a beginning in the remote past. The search for Baptist origins is a formidable task. One of the problems is that Baptists have generally been more concerned with the quality of their present spiritual living than with the past and, therefore, have not imagined that they were people of destiny. For the most part, the early Baptists gave no thought to making a long-range contribution to future generations. As a result, they did not write very much at all, so the literature is minimal. These believers were given all kinds of names—mostly derogatory—by those outside their numbers. The believers cherished their freedom and individuality, and so again they could not see the preservation of their actions as significant to the future. What information is available, therefore, must come from conjecture and from the writings of those who came in contact with the early Baptists.

While realizing that a high level of validity and reliability is not possible for proving any of the theories of Baptist origin, it is worthwhile to explore the stream of humanity from the Gospels to the seventeenth century to find groups holding the Baptist views. After the early 1600s, there is statistical and narrative history from which a more accurate picture may be constructed.

The first theory of the origin of Baptists may be called the *Apostolic Church Successionist Theory*. There is a great difference between the concept of apostolic succession in Roman Catholicism and the concept of church succession. The apostolic age passed with the death of the apostles, but the church of the apostles continued on after their deaths. The basic idea of apostolic church succession is that God never let His lamp of truth go out in the world and, therefore, a church much like that of the New Testament has existed in every age. This theory suggests that these groups of people, by whatever name they might have been called, were among the sects and heretics attacked by the Roman church. (Heretic is used here in the historical sense, meaning those who did not agree with the doctrines of the Roman church.)

Probably the most widely read book holding this successionist view is *The Trail of Blood* by J. M. Carroll, a leader among Southern Baptists. His study of church history led him to note that most of what had been written was about Catholics and

Protestants. In Clarence Walker's introduction to the book, he recounts Carroll's observation that the history of Baptists was "written in blood." Other writers saw this succession in different ways, but Carroll's view has had the widest acceptance because it allows for the addition of two of the other theories to be discussed here. In his huge work *The History of Baptists*, Thomas Armitage goes to great lengths to justify the Apostolic Church Successionist view as the only legitimate possibility without calling it a theory. So this type of successionist theory has significant backing.

Simply stated, the Apostolic Church Successionist theory proposes that Baptists began with either John the Baptist or Jesus Christ. Hiscox, in his *New Directory for Baptist Churches*, states:

> And though, in the dim, uncertain light of subsequent ages of error and corruption, we cannot at all times follow their [the Baptists'] trail, or identify their presence with absolute certainty, yet we feel positively assured that they have always existed. Like a stream which pursues its way from the mountains to the sea, and never ceases, though its course at times be through mountain gorges, trackless deserts, and hidden caverns, we know it is somewhere, though we cannot trace it, but we recognize it when again it comes to light, with a grander sweep, a deeper current, and a stronger tide.[1]

Indeed, the stream of the true church wandered through the ages from the second century through the sixteenth century in the form of Messalians, Montanists, Euchites, Novatians, Donatists, Paulicians, Paterines, Albigenses, Waldenses, Vaudois, Cathari and Poor Men of Lyons—nearly all of which were called *Anabaptists* by their adversaries because they rejected infant baptism and practiced believer's baptism.

It seems, however, quite important to apply more than the believer's baptism criteria to these groups if they are to be considered Baptist. In the first and second centuries, the small but growing groups were given names by outsiders which

1. Hiscox, *New Directory for Baptist Churches*, 494.

either described that group's beliefs and practices or were an adaptation of a chief leader's name. The Messalians and Euchites apparently represent a common view, but the first was a western name and the second an eastern one. The only thing these two groups had in common with the Baptist Distinctives was believer's baptism and a saved church membership. These groups believed that everyone was possessed from his birth by a demon who incited him to sin. Baptism did not remove the demon root, it merely sheared it off. The only way the demon root could be expelled from the person was by intense and perpetual prayer until the evil spirit was seen to leave the individual. They used the symbolism of a sow with her litter as the evil spirit leaving via the person's mouth. Then the Holy Spirit would come as a harmless fire, after which the believer would be at peace with God in the same way an earthly bride is at peace in the embraces of her husband.

The Montanists also began in the first century in Mysia with a dominant leader named Montanus. Montanus claimed to be a prophet who received "truth" directly from God and became the sole spokesman of Jesus Christ. He received his prophetic utterances while in a state of ecstasy. He also had a couple of priestesses (Maximilla and Prisca) who left their husbands and followed Montanus, exhibiting prophetic charisma. Other than these kinds of innovations in religious practice, the Montanists apparently accepted the basic tenets of the New Testament church. The exact end of this group is assumed to have occurred with the unknown dates of the deaths of its leaders, but Tertullian was somewhat identified with them, and his death is believed to have occurred about A.D. 230.

The Novatians, or Novatianists, originated in the third century under the leadership of Novatian. Novatian was a very significant theologian in Rome and was the leading candidate for bishop there. He became involved in a dispute over whether a Christian who returned to paganism (for the sake of saving his human life) could ever be restored to church fellowship and membership upon evidence of repentance. Novatian took the position that the fallen one must have a tested penitence before he could be restored. A disputed bishop in Rome took the opposite view that the church had no power to forgive sin at all. Because of this dispute, Novatian and his followers left the church, either voluntarily or by force. Apparently, although no great amounts of information are available, they accepted most of the Orthodox views, because at the Council of Nicaea (A.D. 325) the Novatian bishops were invited to return to the church at Rome. Just how accurately the Novatians could be judged on the basis of Baptist Distinctives is quite unknown.

The Donatists became predominant during the fourth and fifth centuries. They were located basically in North Africa and their numbers exceeded the Catholics there. The basic differences between Catholics and Donatists came to a head when Donatus began rebaptizing those who had been baptized as babies by the Catholics and reordaining bishops after they had split from the Catholic church. Donatism was not a violation of Catholic teaching; rather, it was a reaction to the increasing secularization as the Catholic church was becoming a "mixed" company of "vessels both for honour and dishonour."

The Paulicians were influential late in the sixth century and into the seventh. They were strong in eastern Europe and influenced the western part. Their durability in spite of disfavor and persecution is attested to by their existence until the twelfth century. These people believed that God had sent an angel to be born of a woman and this angel entered into Sonship at the baptism. They required a forty-day waiting period between what was called believing and baptism into membership. During these forty days the penitent was to fast. They further rejected the worship of Mary and the different clothing by which the priesthood was set apart from the people. They also carried many of the other views of the Baptists which were to follow.

The Albigenses, who existed from the sixth through the sixteenth centuries, originated in the city of Albi, in southern France. Theirs is a history of terrible persecutions and dispersions. After dispersion, their beliefs and practices were carried on under the name Waldenses. Actually, which name they bore depended on the geographic location. The basic conflict with Catholicism did not come to a great confrontation until

1206. The dispute involved the Albigensian denial of the mass and transubstantiation, which they believed were idolatrous and unscriptural; their belief that the Catholic church was not the wife or bride of Christ; and their teaching that the polity of the Roman church had "pernicious and wicked" tendencies. In that year, the armies of Pope Innocent III (assuming the records are reasonably accurate) killed about 200,000 Waldenses, the rest escaping to numerous points of refuge. These Waldenses cherished the distinct doctrine and practice of Christian liberty and generally agreed with what have come to be called the Baptist Distinctives. They might well have been called the Baptists of an early day.

We will not discuss the Paterines, Vaudois, Cathari and Poor Men of Lyons, since basically these groups were smaller offshoots of some of the larger groups.

The Apostolic Church Successionist theory of Baptist origin contains certain strains of truth. Most of the groups carried forward some part of the New Testament beliefs and practices, but few, if any, carried them all. However, the ability to apply the test of Baptist Distinctives to these groups is limited by the availability of viable information.

The second theory of Baptist origin is called the *Anabaptist Kinship Theory*. Many of the Anabaptists were located in Holland, Germany, Switzerland and Wales. Actually, the word "ana-baptist" is a compound word meaning "re-baptizers." They were being ridiculed because they refused to accept the baptism of the unsaved as valid and insisted that believer's baptism was necessary for membership. The name was given to many groups and can only be understood in the light of the Apostolic Church Successionist view, for several of the Anabaptist groups took that basic position. While many of the groups returned to sprinkling as the mode of baptism and baptizing infants (pedo-baptism), most practiced some form of believer's immersion.

The Anabaptists of northern Europe basically held to the Baptist Distinctives discussed in chapter 2. A problem, however, developed through the years as fanatics infiltrated their ranks. The "mad men of Munster," for example, practiced excesses and brought a reproach upon the Anabaptists that they did not deserve. It is common for men to emphasize faults as a means of stirring up negative sentiments against their objects of hatred.

In Holland and Germany, the Anabaptists were led by Menno Simons, and this group came to be known as Mennonites. In Switzerland, the Anabaptists were led by Ulrich Zwingli, and this group has come to be known as the Brethren and the Reformed Church. In Wales, under the leadership of men named Penry, Wroth, Erbury and Powell, late in the Reformation period, the first group emerged that is known to have dropped the prefix "ana" and become known only as Baptists. After that, the group seems to have gotten lost in the many problems that were engulfing the British kingdom.

There is little question that some of the Anabaptist groups fit the basic tenets of Baptist uniqueness. However, because of the wide application of the name to nearly all who rejected sprinkling and/or baptism of infants, it is necessary that great discretion be used in making connections. It does remain, however, that the massive persecutions the Anabaptists suffered for the sake of their faith made a remarkable foundation for Baptist uniqueness.

The third theory of Baptist beginnings is the *English Separatist Descent Theory*. This theory is without question the most adequately defensible. There is ample information in the English language pertaining to this theory. It is actually a part of the Baptist superstructure more than a part of its origin, but it does agree with Hiscox and others who say that we do not need a continuous line of succeeding churches, just so the present-day church is as much like the New Testament church as possible.

This theory makes the Baptists an integral part of the Separatist Movement in England in the sixteenth century. The Baptists therefore have an affinity with the Separatists who were forced to move to Holland and then to the New World as Pilgrims. This theory portrays the early Baptists as persecuted by Catholics, Protestants and Puritans. It also provides the added evidence the Southern Baptists need to finally indicate that Baptists antedate the Reformation and, therefore, are not Protestants.

There is, however, a fourth possibility of Baptist origins.

This theory suggests the *possible existence of baptistic congregations or groups within the Roman Catholic church*. There are both logic and supportive historical data for this theory. We will only be able to give a brief expression of the possibilities, although a longer treatise on this subject could certainly be made.

Stated briefly, it appears that the theological and experiential frameworks of the Roman Catholic church were extremely broad and lenient up to the time of the Protestant Reformation. With the coming of the tremendous challenge by the Protestants, the Roman church was forced to redefine its position and make some of its "unofficial" practices and beliefs the official dogma of the church. These Catholic reforms were made mainly at the Council of Trent in the late sixteenth century. This looseness of Roman Catholic framework could have allowed people who held Baptistic views to remain within the Catholic fold. However, when the restrictions of Trent became enforceable on all assemblies about 1600, the separatist Baptists could no longer stay in the Catholic church, and soon thereafter Baptists appear on the pages of history.

From the beginning of the institution called the church until the time of the emperor Constantine (fourth century), each local church was essentially free to decide its own doctrine and practice. Some churches sprinkled babies as early as A.D. 150. Some Novatian churches used pouring as baptism. Novatian himself was baptized as a believing adult by pouring. History records that he was ill and perhaps about to die, but he had not been baptized. Unable to be immersed, as was the approved way, his followers poured water all around and over him on his bed as a form of baptism. He subsequently was restored to health, and the question was raised about the appropriateness of his baptism by pouring. The decision was that it actually did not matter how much water was used just as long as the participant was a believer at the time. Because differing modes of baptism were used in the churches, it is apparent that no one way was a specific requirement. However, some form of baptism was required for membership.

There was no *official* church bureaucratic hierarchy at this time. Each local church had its own bishop (pastor). It was, however, quite normal for certain pastors to gain higher recognition than others, and thus it developed that certain bishops became highly respected by other pastors in the same geographic area. The pastors now had a pastor or bishop. The question arises, "Who was the bishop's bishop?" The answer ultimately is that the bishop at Rome was the prominent one, and the idea of the papacy was born. The papacy was, as is true in many institutions, created for the sake of expediency. Although practical to some degree, the Roman church did not fully dogmatize the papacy until it established papal infallibility in 1870.

All through the Middle Ages, the Roman church practiced a number of things with which baptistic people could not agree. However, the Roman church persecuted only those who threatened its hierarchy. Baptistic people were basically non-militant and as a result would not challenge state or church systems as long as they could worship as they believed.

The Renaissance found the Roman church extremely weak and ineffective in protecting itself. Its seminary and university professors had begun accepting humanistic views. They would sign the required doctrinal statement of the church with tongue in cheek and then teach humanism with no tinge of conscience. Others, like Savonarola, openly asked what right the popes had to the authority they used. True, many were martyred for the causes they espoused, but the point here is that many questions were now being openly asked. The Roman church was in serious difficulty.

Martin Luther and the other leaders of the Protestant Reformation definitely got the full attention of the church. Actually, the Protestants did not wish to destroy the Roman church; they wanted to change it only minimally. What the Reformation served to do, however, was cause the Roman Catholic leaders to make significant definitive rules about church belief and practice. The Protestants refer to this time of rule making as the Counter Reformation, while the Catholics refer to it as the Catholic Reformation.

For our purposes, we will discuss only the decisions of the Council of Trent (1545-1563), for they well illustrate the possibilities of this theory of Baptists coming out of the Catholic church. It is noteworthy that each of the council's decisions rendered many things *official* that had been believed and practiced *unofficially* (and, therefore, were unenforceable) during the growth of the Roman Catholic church. Here is a list of some of the dogmas that were to be accepted by all Roman churches after the Council of Trent:

1. The Holy Scripture, including the Apocrypha, was to be accepted in the Latin Vulgate alone.
2. Unwritten traditions given by Christ to the apostles, and which have been in continuous succession preserved in the Roman Catholic church, were to be followed.
3. No one could rely upon his own skill in interpreting the Scriptures in any sense other than the sense that the Mother Church held.
4. What man lost in the Fall did not totally destroy his free will, it merely weakened it.
5. The Virgin Mary was excluded from the operation of original sin. (In 1854, this was more clearly defined by papal decree in the form of the Immaculate Conception, that is, Mary being born without sin, and the actual deification of Mary.)
6. No one can know for certain during his earthly life whether he is one of God's chosen ones.
7. A system of penance was to be administered to aid in restoring those fallen from grace.
8. The seven sacraments (Baptism, Confirmation, Penance, the Holy Eucharist, Marriage, Extreme Unction and Holy Orders) are of varying value but are necessary in obtaining grace unto salvation.
9. Transubstantiation occurs during the Holy Eucharist. (That is, when the priest blesses the bread and wine, they become the substance of Christ's body and blood.)
10. Confession of sins (to a priest) was to be required for participation in the Eucharist.
11. Extreme Unction (or Last Rites) was to be performed by a priest at a specified time prior to death.
12. The Mass was to be propitiatory for both the living and the dead. It was to be celebrated only by the priests

and not in the language of the people. However, occasionally parts of it should be expounded so that the members could understand.

13. The ordained priesthood was to be the only true priesthood (thereby declaring the priesthood of all believers to be false).

14. Only ordained priests were to have the authority to consecrate and administer the sacraments and to forgive any remaining sins.

15. Marriage was to be indissoluble.

16. Celibacy and virginity were not to be inferior to marriage.

17. Saints in Heaven were to be asked to intercede with God the Father through Jesus Christ on behalf of men on earth and in purgatory.

18. Abuses of an unedifying or mercenary nature of relics, images and indulgences were to be stopped.

19. All church dignitaries and teachers were to take an oath acknowledging the Roman church as the Mother and Mistress of Churches, promising to obey the bishop as the successor of Saint Peter and the vicar of Christ, accepting the canons and decrees of the church (including the Council of Trent) and promising life-long adherence to the true Catholic faith without which no one can be saved.

It is improbable that these enforcements were made at the close of the Council of Trent on December 4, 1563. It is very likely that it took some time, at least, for the implementation. It would seem, however, that any who held the Baptist viewpoint would no longer be able to remain in the Roman Catholic church and would have to separate from it.

Something else was happening in England during the sixteenth century reign of Queen Elizabeth I and later under James I. One of the directives of the Church of England, a Protestant church, was that all "nonconformists" were to leave the country. A nonconformist was anyone who did not agree to the positions of the Church of England. Many English Separatists went to Amsterdam for the sake of their personal convictions and their lives. One of these was a man named John

Smyth. He had been loyal to the Church of England but had found areas of concern. Voicing these concerns classified him as a nonconformist who must leave the kingdom. In Holland, he studied diligently and began writing and distributing his findings. Of primary interest was his rejection of the Roman Catholic and Anglican position on baptism. He began teaching and practicing the baptism of believers-only by immersion. There are some stories that Mr. Smyth immersed himself upon his conviction of believer's immersion, but these may only have been rumors. He and his followers organized themselves into a local church with the distinctive Baptist traits.

Such was the beginning of the first actual Baptist church of English-speaking people, and it started in Holland. Mr. Smyth died sometime between 1610 and 1612, and it remained for Thomas Helwys to lead the formation of the Baptist churches on English soil during the approximate years 1612 to 1614. By that time it had become reasonably safe for the nonconformists to return.

These are the four possible avenues in the search for the origin of the people called Baptists. Whether any of these is wholly acceptable is open for substantial debate. The fact does remain, however, that God never allowed the lamp of His truth to be extinguished, and He will carefully see to it that for all of this Age of Grace there will be a people for His Name.

4

The Meaning and Chronological Order of Baptist Associations

Like sore thumbs, the Demases, the Alexanders, the Diotrophes get more notice. We need to campaign to spotlight the far greater number of steadfast, unmovable saints of whom the world is not worthy.

Churches—every one of them—preaching the Word. Churches reaching out, seeking the lost. Churches sending forth missionary volunteers. Churches trying to hold a standard of holiness in a society that has abandoned righteousness. Churches struggling to maintain purity of doctrine and polity.

Indeed, not one of them is perfect. They all have their percentage of carnal Christians. Some are torn by dissension, as was Corinth and probably Philippi. All could be doing a better job. Some don't show much life. . . .

But, on the whole, they bear evidence of God's transforming grace.[1]

—Merle R. Hull

One aspect of Baptist uniqueness has been its position on local church sovereignty as discussed in chapter 2.

---

1. Merle R. Hull, *What a Fellowship! The First Fifty Years of the General Association of Regular Baptist Churches* (Schaumburg, IL: Regular Baptist Press, 1981), 65-66.

Baptists treasure their independence so much that many of them specifically title their churches "Independent Baptist." Technically, this is unnecessary because the historic use of the term "Baptist" means a local church owns and operates itself independent of external control and influence.

These local Baptist churches often have members who tend to think independently also. As a believer-priest, each has the freedom to discover God's will through the study of the Scriptures, praying and weighing the circumstances. It is only through these avenues that he should express what he believes to be correct in the business of the church. Done in a spirit of love, care and respect for other believers, this process can be a very spiritual experience. Sadly, selfishness and human egotism often stand in the way, and the testimony of the church becomes minimized in the community. There are times when the Bible is abused and rejected even in Baptist churches, and separation and division may be the necessary result. Many devisive elements in churches have very little to do with anything spiritual but rather are carnally human. Some instances of separations will be studied in later chapters.

Perhaps this independent spirit and behavior is partly responsible for the rather small sizes of memberships in Baptist churches. True, there are some huge Baptist churches, especially in the South, but if we use the data provided by Frank Mead in his *Handbook of Denominations in the United States* (1980), we can illustrate that the average church membership is small:

> Southern Baptist Convention 370
> American Baptist Churches 270
> Conservative Baptist Association 270
> Baptist General Conference 170
> General Association of Regular Baptists 150
> North American Baptist Conference 150
> Freewill Baptists 100

There may be several reasons for such small churches. First, as we have already seen, the independent spirit may cause division. Second, Baptists have historically been evangelistic in small communities. It is very difficult to build a local church of one thousand members if only five hundred people are in the constituency, and there may be five or more denominations "competing" for their share. Third, Baptist indigenous practices tend to define "local" in a rather narrow sense. For instance, one local church determined that it would not deliberately try to work with people outside a fifteen square mile area because there were about twenty thousand people within three or four miles of the church building. A church cannot forbid people to come from greater distances, of course, but the church reaching and reflecting its immediate community is a Baptist trademark. Fourth, Baptist home missionary practices aim at encouraging present members to go out and begin churches in surrounding areas. Therefore, there is some depletion of members for the sake of evangelism and church planting. Certainly there are other reasons strong or weak, valid or invalid, pleasant or unpleasant, for which churches remain small. It may also be wise to point out that a large membership does not necessarily indicate spiritual success. When godly people give their testimonies, they often mention a small church somewhere in their background in which a truly spiritual work was being done. A poet once wrote a long poem called, "God Bless the Little Churches."

Of course, the small size of the average Baptist church presents some limitations. With the coming of modern foreign missions, it has become very costly to put missionaries on a field for four years or more. One small church could not completely support a missionary. It requires some cooperation, and therefore mission agencies have come into operation. Also, there are times when churches must work together in the promotion of a large-scale cause or defense against a widespread threat.

There are many ways of working together cooperatively, but Baptists have employed their independent, congregational approach to these unions. They have called them *associations*. The basic idea of an association is that individual local churches choose to fellowship together with no thought of any local church, or the association as a whole, controlling any other local church. The key words for historic Baptists were

"voluntary" and "fellowship." These associations are significant only in that they provide strength to accomplish some
things that could not be done by each church separately.

J. Irving Reese, in his *Guide for Organizing and Conducting a Baptist Church*, discusses church relationships:

> While local churches may not "federate" they do
> "associate," that is, they fellowship in organizations
> for the more effective promotion of Gospel work.
> Churches do not "join" these organizations, but
> merely declare themselves to be in "fellowship"
> with them; nor are their representatives to the
> meetings of these organizations considered to be
> "delegates," but "messengers." They have no au-
> thority to act for the church but merely to bear
> fraternal greetings, join in the discussions and busi-
> ness, and report their findings back to the *local* as-
> sembly, which is in no manner bound by the actions
> of the larger body or by any pledges made by its
> own messengers.
>
> In Baptist circles, there are usually *three* larger
> organizations with which the local church may fel-
> lowship: (1)the *local Association*, now sometimes called
> "Fellowship," or "Bible Conference." This includes
> churches in a comparatively small area which are
> easily accessible to each other, as those of a city
> and/or county; (2)the *State Association*; and (3) the *Na-
> tional Association*. Each of these associations is in-
> dependent of the other two and a church need not
> fellowship with any unless it desires to do so, or may
> be in one and not in the others. Experience has
> proved, however, that *there is great spiritual and practical
> value in such associations*. A church should refrain from
> declaring itself in fellowship with *two associations on the
> same territorial level*, as such dual relationship may
> prove confusing both to the church and the associa-
> tion affected.[2]

2. Reese, *Guide for Organizing a Baptist Church*, 39-40.

It is also relevant to quote extensively from Hiscox's *New Directory for Baptist Churches* regarding church associations:

There is at times no little confusion of thought occasioned by want of a clear understanding as to the true nature and real purpose of *Associations*; and that, too, by ministers themselves, who ought to be able expounders of Baptist polity and usage. Especially as to the relations which these bodies sustain to the churches; whether they can act *for* the associated churches, and in some sense bind them by their action.

It is customary for churches occupying a given extent of territory—usually less than a State, perhaps limited portions of contiguous States, not so widely extended as to make it difficult, because of distance, to meet in one place, nor yet embracing so many churches as to make the meetings inconveniently large—by common agreement to organize on some simple basis of association for mutual helpfulness and counsel.

These churches agree to cooperate in the Association, and meet yearly with some one of them, by their pastors, and a certain number of members, appointed as *messengers*. These meetings usually hold two days, sometimes more, and the time is occupied in hearing reports from various churches —each one sending with the messengers a letter, setting forth their condition as to anything of special interest to themselves or to the body. Sermons are preached, prayer-meetings held, and various matters pertaining to the prosperity of the cause come under consideration. Missionary work on their field is fostered, new churches are planted, and weak ones aided. . . .

These annual gatherings constitute not only favorable opportunities for projecting plans for missionary work within the bounds of the Association, but they also give occasion for pleasant fraternal intercourse on the part of members of the various churches, who, at these Christian festivals, form and foster personal friendships of a most pleasant and profitable character. This is particularly true in rural districts, where they have few opportunities for personal intercourse.[3]

On the next eight pages of his *New Directory*, Hiscox gives nine observations, summarized as follows:

1. The term "association" has two uses: one, an organized, corporate body, consisting of pastors and messengers, meeting periodically for the transaction of business, publishing its proceedings for its membership; two, the geographic limits over which the represented associated churches are scattered.

2. An association meeting for business is *not* composed of churches, but individuals—pastors and messengers. A Baptist *church* cannot be a member of another body because to do so would violate its sacred charter as a sovereign local church.

3. Churches are not "received into *membership*," although such expressions are frequently and ordinarily used, but they are received into *fellowship* and *cooperation*; their pastors and appointed messengers are those actually accepted into the membership of the association for transaction of business.

4. An association is not a body of messengers gathered to do business on behalf of their churches. A local church cannot transfer its authority and responsibility to any other person or group of persons meeting outside itself.

5. An association is a *voluntary* society. It is humanly, not divinely, established. No church is obligated to affiliate, and members may withdraw from the fellowship for any reason sufficient to themselves. Members must, however, live by the rules mutually agreed upon.

6. An association cannot legislate for the churches, exercise any authority over the churches, or bind the churches to any conformity whatsoever. The association may make suggestions to churches or request from

3. Hiscox, *New Directory*, 330-332.

churches, but each individual church must decide the extent to which it will be involved.

7. The appointment by a local church of a messenger to an association carries with it no ecclesiastical authority.

8. An association is a sovereign, independent body, framing its own rules and purposes. It is no more to be controlled by the churches than the churches are to be controlled by it. If a church does not approve of the actions of an association, it can choose not to affiliate; or if already in association, it can withdraw.

9. An association has full responsibility for refusing or receiving messengers from churches. Provisions for acceptance or rejection of messengers are located in the mutually developed constitution.[4]

A question often asked is, What is the difference between an association and a convention? Baptists did not use the term "convention" until 1845, when many Baptists in the South wished to form a cooperative effort. Initially, a convention referred only to an assembling of messengers from churches from a larger geographic base—usually a state or nation. The composition of these conventions varied and were indefinite. As conventionism grew, a number of changes occurred. Perhaps most significant was the appointment of an *executive secretary*, in whom was entrusted a great amount of power and influence, if not control, over the local churches in the convention. There appears to be much more of a hierarchical direction in a convention than in an association. Although Baptists have historically shunned this type of union, there were two instances when Baptist associations entrusted direction of societies and agencies to a select few: the Southern Baptist Convention (1845) and the Northern Baptist Convention (1907).

With this rather lengthy introduction, we will now examine the history of Baptist associations in a chronological fashion. There have been literally hundreds, if not thousands, of Baptist associations, so we will discuss only a select, and hopefully

4. Ibid., 332-339.

representative, few from the seventeenth century to the present time.

Accord.... to *The Baptist Encyclopedia* (1883), the first Baptist association was formed around Somersetshire, England, in 1653. The first association on a national scale was organized in London in September 1689 (although the preface of the Confession developed there says July 1689). Messengers from more than a hundred churches in England and Wales gathered. The encyclopedia says that this convention (they called themselves an association) disclaimed all "power to prescribe or impose anything upon the faith or practice of any of the churches of Christ," and further, "that whatever is determined by us in any case shall not be binding upon any one church till the consent of that church first be had."[5] The minutes are reportedly filled with counsel and advice which was "proved out of the Word of God."[6] This gathering took place when travel was very expensive and dangerous for the messengers, so the meetings thereafter were on a smaller, more localized scale. This London assembly produced a valuable document that has been influential ever since—*the Philadelphia Confession of Faith*. According to the preface, the purpose of this confession was to inform Baptist congregations and "other Christians" what things were generally believed and practiced "for the glory of God." Thirty-seven signatures are affixed to this historic document.

The first association in America was the Philadelphia Association in 1707. The next oldest in order were:

The Charleston (South Carolina) Association—1751

The Sandy Creek (North Carolina) Association—1758

The Kehukee (North Carolina) Association—1765

The Ketocton (Virginia) Association—1766

The Warren (Rhode Island) Association—1767

The Stonington (Connecticut) Association—1772

The Red Stone (Pennsylvania) Association—1776

5. William Cathcart, *The Baptist Encyclopedia* (Philadelphia: Louis H. Everts, 1883), 46.
6. Ibid.

The New Hampshire (New Hampshire) Association—
  1776
The Shaftesbury (Vermont) Association—1781
The Woodstock (Vermont) Association—1783
The Georgia (Georgia) Association—1784
The Holston (Tennessee) Association—1786
The Bowdoinham (Maine) Association—1787
The Vermont (Vermont) Association—1787

By the mid-1800s there were over one thousand associations in the United States alone. Each group reflected a special characteristic in its origin or practice, indicating a wide variety of Baptists. Perhaps this individual uniqueness is another indicator of the separatist tendencies that brought about the initial formation of the Baptists as a whole.

1611—GENERAL BAPTISTS

This is the first group of Baptists with a definitive identification. Initially there were very few churches begun by Helwys and Smyth in England and Holland. Roger Williams was the first General Baptist preacher in America. Theologically, the General Baptists were Arminian, emphasizing man's free will to be saved, and they were considerably frustrated when they encountered the much stronger Calvinistic views in the Middle Colonies. The group nearly died out but was revived and formed a renewed association in Illinois and Kentucky in 1870. Since that time, they have grown and now have approximately nine hundred churches in at least sixteen states. They have one liberal arts college which includes a theology department, and they support missionary activity mostly in the South Pacific and in the United States.

General Baptists are congregational in polity with local associations forming a larger General Association. All associational relationships are representative and advisory only. They do have one unusual practice for a Baptist group: they use a form of presbytery on the local associational level. The presbytery examines candidates for the ministry and for deacon, and once these are ordained they are responsible to the examining presbytery.

1644—PARTICULAR BAPTISTS

The Particular Baptists began in England, but unlike the General Baptists who separated from the Church of England, they were more ecumenical. They were less protesting and more independent from the beginning. Their position was that the Anglicans were not entirely corrupt, and neither were some other groups, so they sought fellowship with them. Also, rebaptism was not a prerequisite for membership in their churches.

The Particular Baptists included some interesting people in their formative years: Henry Jacob, the founder, who was considerably influenced by John Robinson, the pastor of the Pilgrim church in Amsterdam and later in Leyden; and one Praise-God Barebone, a leather salesman, member of Parliament and pastor. Barebone took over the ministry of one-half of Jacob's church, holding regular meetings in his house. He had originally held to infant baptism but later accepted the position on believer's baptism held by most Baptist groups.

The theology of the Particular Baptists was much more Calvinistic than the General Baptists, as their London Confession indicates. In their case, this theological position kept them from much evangelistic interest. It also led them to a more authoritarian stance in church government, encouraged their associational ties and allowed for some control from outside the congregation.

During the eighteenth century, the Particular Baptists spent much of their time in disputings, organization and being generally censorious. This is an important fact because it kept them from being a part of the spiritual awakening so deeply needed in England at that time. Instead of evangelizing, they spent great sums of money to build fine church buildings. As the local churches became more self-centered, the ministers worked only within the immediate environs of the church building. They seem to have been most intent on promotional schemes to get the money from the members to pay the higher costs. A kind of theological or ecclesiastical spell fell upon them, keeping them from evangelistic concern. Attendance and membership began to decline.

It is ironic that a moderate Calvinistic preacher of a Particular Baptist church in Northamptonshire was used to greatly influence one of his young parishioners toward missionary activity—William Carey. As a result, the first Baptist foreign mission society was established.

During the nineteenth century, the Particular Baptists became divided into three groups: strict Calvinist, closed communionist and open evangelistic. Associational life grew in the desire to gain strength for each position. It was through some of the Particular Baptist groups that the Calvinistic doctrines came to the Middle Colonies in America beginning as early as 1730. The Particular Baptists have been a strong influence on many of the Baptist groups of the South.

Particular Baptist lethargy in evangelism led to the formation in about 1863 of a new group called the Baptist Union. This group drew from many varieties of Baptists who were interested in spreading the gospel. Probably one of the best-known preachers typifying the union's approach was Charles Haddon Spurgeon. For all practical purposes, the Particular Baptists as an association were no longer effective by the mid-nineteenth century.

1672—SEVENTH-DAY BAPTIST GENERAL CONFERENCE

The unique mark of this group is its belief in and practice of the seventh day, or sabbath, as its day of worship. They were called Sabbatarians in England. When Stephen Mumford came to Rhode Island, he fellowshiped with two other churches of the same persuasion and thus formed the Seventh-Day Baptist General Conference. Today there are about sixty churches in this group, and they have a united effort in missions known as Our World Mission. The conference participates in the modern ecumenical movement at all levels. There is a Seventh-Day Baptist World Federation which includes conferences from Africa, Central and South America and the South Pacific.

1695—SEPARATE BAPTISTS IN CHRIST

This group was begun in America by some refugees from

the Separatist persecutions in England. They were mildly Calvinistic and strongly influenced by the powerful, revivalistic preaching of George Whitefield.

This group is set apart by its practice of three ordinances: baptism by immersion, the Lord's Supper and foot washing. Their associational life is advisory only, and unified missionary activity is limited to a small home missionary effort and one full-time missionary in Africa. Individuals and churches may, and do, support other missionary and outreach ventures.

Mergers and union with other Baptist groups depleted their numbers through the years, but approximately eighty of these churches are still known to exist. Their extreme separation makes statistics difficult to locate.

1727—FREEWILL BAPTISTS

When the Arminian Baptists migrated to the American colonies from England, they were very independent from each other. A southern group organized in 1727 under the leadership of Paul Palmer in North Carolina. Later, in 1780, a northern line was formed under the leadership of Benjamin Randall in New Hampshire. Although both groups practiced the doctrines of free grace, free salvation and free will, attempts at union were disrupted by the Civil War. Most of the northern group merged with the Northern Baptist Convention in 1910. The southern group reorganized at least twice, presently being in the form of the National Association of Freewill Baptists. They have about 2500 churches in forty states.

1787—UNITED BAPTISTS

This group is a unique union of Baptists of the Regular Baptist tradition and the Separatist Baptist tradition on a small scale. There is great variety among them: individualistic preaching styles, open and closed communion, and some practice foot washing as an ordinance. Although many of their members have gone on to Northern and Southern Baptist churches, they still have nearly six hundred churches, located mostly in the border states.

1820—TWO-SEED-IN-THE-SPIRIT
PREDESTINARIAN BAPTISTS

A close connection with the Waldenses is seen in this group of Baptists. This association began in Virginia under the leadership of Elder Daniel Parker, who published the *Church Advocate* paper. They were extreme Calvinists with some unusual twists: (1) the belief that two seeds were planted in Eve, one by God and one by Satan, every baby being born with one seed or the other; (2) the endowing of a minister with "legal authority" through the laying on of hands by the presbytery; (3) the rejection of a paid clergy; (4) the uselessness of missions; and (5) the acceptance of foot washing as an ordinance.

Their numbers, although never very large, have diminished seriously. Lack of unity in reporting makes data hard to find, but the latest report found was from 1945, at which time there were only sixteen churches with a total membership of 201.

1825—DUCK RIVER ASSOCIATION OF BAPTISTS

This group is located in Alabama, Tennessee, Mississippi and Georgia with about one hundred churches, nearly all of which are small. The association developed out of a controversy over the importance of missions and the operation of a Christian school in what was called the Elk River Association. Other dissenters in the struggle became known as Missionary Baptists.

Doctrinally, the Duck River Association is quite Calvinistic with a strong idea of perseverance toward obtaining saving grace. They also practice foot washing as an ordinance. Interestingly, ministers are provided through an ordination conducted by two (or more) already ordained men.

1845—SOUTHERN BAPTIST CONVENTION

The struggle regarding slavery began many years before the Civil War, and it perhaps was inevitable that the differing viewpoints would affect Baptist churches in America. The headquarters of the Baptist Foreign Mission Board was located in Boston and its leadership was strongly influenced by abolitionists. A decision was made to exclude slave-holders from being accepted as missionaries. With a common budget and fund for missionary enterprises, the southern churches resented that *their* missionaries could not be supported by *their* money. In May 1845 the Southern Baptist Convention was formed, and the members immediately established their own board for foreign and home missions.

Although the missions problem caused the ultimate break, there was another powerful difference between Baptist churches in the North and South. The churches of the North were committed to very independent local churches with little, if any, denominational organization directing missionary societies and social agencies. In the South, however, there was a strong desire for centralized control of such societies and agencies.

Mead's *Handbook of Denominations* gives some interesting statistics about the Southern Baptists:

  1845—351,951 members (130,000 were blacks)
  1890—1,235,908 members (all of them whites)
  1972—12,067,284 members (both black and white
  affiliated congregations)[7]

Southern Baptists today hold a conservative theology, but basically they adhere to similar beliefs and practices of the Baptists in the North. Although Southern Baptists are quite Calvinistic, they are involved in home and foreign missions (they have about three thousand missionaries abroad), are avid supporters of Sunday Schools and are heavily involved in publications, educational enterprises and social agencies. The Sunday School board of the convention provides material for over seven million students in more than 34,000 Sunday Schools.

In recent years, this rapidly growing convention has been establishing churches in the North and holding its annual con-

7. Frank S. Mead, *Handbook of Denominations in the United States* (Nashville: Parthenon Press, 1980), 34-58.

vention outside the South. This leads some to conclude that it is no longer just a southern group but a national group.

1851—NORTH AMERICAN BAPTIST CONFERENCE

The North American Baptist Conference began after a number of German immigrants settled in Pennsylvania and established some churches there between 1840 and 1850. The Quakers there were friendly and fostered the religious freedom needed for this Baptist movement to get underway. In 1851, the eight churches that were operating organized into an association. Today there are about 350 churches in the conference scattered over the United States and Canada. The conference as a whole meets every three years, but the several smaller associations meet each year.

This conference is in the mainstream of Baptist positions, accepting the New Hampshire Confession and practicing a strong missions emphasis. The conference participated in the development of what is known as the Colgate-Rochester Divinity School, but in 1935 they began their own school in Sioux Falls, South Dakota. They also are involved in social service through children's homes and homes for the aged.

1852—BAPTIST GENERAL CONFERENCE

Another of the national church groups, the Baptist General Conference began in 1852 in Rock Island, Illinois. A number of Swedish Lutherans, influenced by the Pietist Movement in Sweden, had immigrated to America to be free from their state church (Lutheran). A settlement was established around Rock Island, and Gustaf Palmquist came to be their lay-leader in spiritual things. He came into contact with the Baptists at nearby Galesburg, Illinois, and was baptized and ordained a Baptist minister. Returning to his Swedish flock, he led in the conversion and baptism of some of them into the Baptist faith.

For many years the American Baptist Home Mission Society, and later the Northern Baptist Convention, assisted this group financially. Gradually, however, they became more self-supporting and in 1879 they formed the Swedish Baptist

General Conference of America. Until 1944 their missionary activities were associated with the American Baptist Mission Societies. At that point, the conference set up its own board and began conducting its own missionary program.

After World War I, national conflicts encouraged the churches to stop using the name "Swedish" in their church titles and to decrease the use of the Swedish language in their services. In 1945 the conference changed its name officially to the Baptist General Conference. Since then they have experienced rapid growth in churches, missions and total numbers. They have their own college and seminary (Bethel College and Seminary in St. Paul, Minnesota), children's homes and homes for the aged. They have about 750 churches across America.

More and more, the Baptist General Conference has expanded to include other nationalities in their memberships. In fact, some of their churches have few, if any, Swedes in them, and many of their pastors are not of Swedish heritage.

The conference is theologically conservative, holding strongly to the acceptance of the Word of God as their rule of faith and practice. Although they are very insistent upon their stand regarding the basic Baptist beliefs, they exhibit great respect for individual differences of opinion on peripheral matters.

1901—UNITED FREEWILL BAPTIST CHURCH

This black denominational group organized in 1901 and has most of its churches (about 850) in a few southern states. Its roots are in the Freewill Baptist Church and it holds to the same position and practices. Although they are congregational in government, some of their local autonomy is lost because they carry church disputes to the general conferences for directive settlement.

1905—AMERICAN BAPTIST ASSOCIATION (LANDMARKISM)

The Landmarkists, who began this association in 1905, believed very strongly that the local church was the only unit authorized to carry out the Great Commission. This cherishing of local church sovereignty led some to call them Church-Equality Baptists. The association strongly opposes "modern science," upholds the distinctive Baptist beliefs and teaches absolute freedom of religious exercise in a free state. Associational life is purely fraternal with messengers gathering periodically for mutual encouragement.

The nearly 3600 churches cooperate in supporting home and foreign missions, publications and educational institutions. Although most of their churches are in the rural areas of the South, they have recently begun churches in the North and East, and there is a definite shift from rural to urban orientation in most of their churches.

1907—AMERICAN BAPTIST CHURCHES IN THE USA

Until the Civil War, Baptist activity was carried on basically by local churches with a general cooperative effort in missions. The southern churches, however, formed their own group, leaving the northern Baptist churches also on their own. Plans had already been started for a national body to coordinate all efforts, and when the southern Baptists separated the efforts in the North were pressed to proceed more rapidly.

Three major Baptist organizations became strong in the North: the American Baptist Home Mission Society, the American Baptist Foreign Mission Society and the American Baptist Publication Society. It was believed that these three groups, competing for support, confused the constituency, so the Northern Baptist Convention was organized in 1907 to administer all the work.

In 1950, the name was changed to American Baptist Convention, and in 1972 the convention adopted a new name of American Baptist Churches in the USA. There are about six thousand churches in the organization. State conventions and the national convention give considerable administrative responsibility to the executive secretary at each level, while still technically maintaining local church sovereignty. Strong ties of cooperation are maintained through cooperative mission activity, the ministers and missionaries retirement and insurance program and the publications department.

The organization as a whole is more liberal theologically and philosophically than many Baptist groups. They encourage baptism and the Lord's Supper as aids to the growth of believers, but they are not considered necessary. They became involved in the modernist movement of the early twentieth century and participate in the ecumenical efforts of the National and World Councils of Churches.

1907—NATIONAL PRIMITIVE BAPTIST CONVENTION IN THE USA

This convention is made up totally of black Primitive Baptists, having separated, by mutual consent of the integrated Primitive Baptist churches, during post-Civil War years. They were first called Colored Primitive Baptists, but in 1907 they organized under the name National Primitive Baptist Convention. Their convention is very loose in structure and primarily fraternal because they strongly believe in the autonomy of the local church. In the six hundred or more of their congregations, there is a tendency among the older and more orthodox to resist establishment of Sunday Schools, organizational ties with other churches and other cooperative ventures.

1920—NATIONAL BAPTIST EVANGELICAL LIFE AND SOUL SAVING ASSEMBLY OF THE USA

This group was formed within the National Baptist Convention but became independent as an assembly in 1937. There are about 250 churches affiliated with the organization. They are primarily involved in social concerns and evangelism. One of their unique features is granting degrees for studying correspondence material within 60 to 120 days in "Evangelology, Deaconology, Missionology, Pastorology and Laymanology."

1932—GENERAL ASSOCIATION OF REGULAR BAPTIST CHURCHES

This association formed out of the conflict within the Northern Baptist Convention regarding modernist tendencies.

Twenty-two churches sent pastors and representatives to Chicago in 1932 to form this fundamentalist association. The General Association of Regular Baptist Churches presently includes approximately sixteen hundred fellowshiping churches.

It is an association of *churches*, not allowing individuals to join. Any Baptist church wishing to join the association must withdraw from all other denominational ties. Any cooperative, organizational relationships with modernists or liberals is considered unscriptural. The association has no organizational control over churches, schools, mission agencies or social programs. They do, however, "approve" five independent Baptist home and foreign mission agencies, nine independent colleges and seminaries, three children's agencies, one agency for the mentally retarded and one home for senior citizens. Participation is encouraged in the approved institutions, but there is no unified budget supporting them denominationally.

State associations and the national association are organized with a council of pastors and a state or national representative giving oversight. The sovereignty of local Baptist churches is carefully guarded, the councils and representatives being viewed as servants of the churches. Evangelism, church planting, publications, missions and education are promoted in the movement.

1934—CHRISTIAN UNITY BAPTIST ASSOCIATION

An argument over open and closed communion brought about the formation of this group. There are five churches in this association, practicing open communion as an ordinance, foot washing and a highly revivalistic outreach. This is one of the smallest associations in America.

1934—BETHEL MINISTERIAL ASSOCIATION

This highly revivalistic, independent group was formed in southern Indiana with about twenty-five churches participating. They are extremely separatist and prefer not to have their positions published generally. Information can be gained individually from their Evansville, Indiana, headquarters.

1935—GENERAL CONFERENCE OF THE EVANGELICAL BAPTIST CHURCH, INC.

A problem arose among the Freewill Baptists which led to the formation of this conference in 1935. They had formerly been called the Church of the Full Gospel but did not formally become a separate conference until they changed their name to the General Conference of the Evangelical Baptist Church, Inc. There was apparently a strong influence by the Wesleyans among them which caused the difference in view between them and the Freewill Baptists. They hold to all the other beliefs of the Freewill Baptists, their conference organization is nearly identical and they exchange pastors quite freely. There are less than fifty of these churches, mostly in the Appalachian area.

1947—CONSERVATIVE BAPTIST ASSOCIATION

The founders of this group were active in the Baptist Bible Union of the 1920s within the Northern Baptist Convention. The purpose of the union had been to rid the convention of modernists and restore it to the fundamentals of the faith. They believed that they could stay in the convention and "clean it up."

In May 1947, a number of pastors and laymen met in Atlantic City, New Jersey, to form the Conservative Baptist Association. A constitution was framed in 1948. They are conservative in both belief and practice, and they have the Conservative Baptist Home Mission Society, the Conservative Baptist Foreign Mission Society and a number of colleges and seminaries fostering their outreach. Although these organizations are not denominationally controlled, there is a close relationship between them and the churches.

To become a member of the Conservative Baptist Association, an individual or a church does not have to separate from membership in the American Baptist Churches. This attitude allows for a certain amount of dual affiliation, although most members do completely sever those former ties.

Organizationally, the association has national and regional

officers elected at their annual meetings. These directors are elected for three-year terms, but they serve only as a recommending body because the association holds the sovereignty of the local church as part of its doctrine. There are approximately twelve hundred churches in the association, located in most areas of the country.

1950—BAPTIST MISSIONARY ASSOCIATION

The organization of this association took place in Little Rock, Arkansas, in 1950 under the name of the North American Baptist Association, but the present name was taken in 1968. As its name suggests, its principal thrust is missionary activity. There are about fifteen hundred churches with about twenty missionaries in Europe, the Far East and Latin America. Theologically they are militant fundamentalists who hold the historic Baptist beliefs while expressing strong negative teaching against open communion, baptism other than in their own churches, labor unions, modernism, pastoral dictatorship, etc.

Each church is completely autonomous, but they cooperate in missions and the operation of four schools and some children's homes.

1950—BAPTIST BIBLE FELLOWSHIP

In the 1940s the World Baptist Fellowship was held each year in Ft. Worth, Texas. It was a conservative reaction to the modernism that had been expanding since the early twentieth century. Led by J. Frank Norris, the World Baptist Fellowship had organized a seminary in his church with financial support from many other churches across the country. Serious tensions arose when pastors of many of these supporting churches felt that they should not be excluded from directing seminary operations. Because of this conflict, about one hundred pastors left the fellowship in 1950 to form the Baptist Bible Fellowship. They also began the Baptist Bible College in Springfield, Missouri.

There are over two thousand churches in the Baptist Bible

Fellowship with well over a million members. It is a loosely organized movement of sovereign Baptist churches, many of which declare themselves "independent" of all affiliations even though their names are in the yearly directory of the fellowship. The fellowship has a thirty-five-member mission board or committee which aids missions in over thirty-two countries.

The churches are primarily very separatist and sometimes isolationist, since they promote a highly militant fundamentalism. Many of their churches are very small, but there are some extremely large and vocal churches numbering as many as twenty thousand members. One of the trademarks of the fellowship has been its emphasis on numbers in attendance, and they were involved early in the "bus ministry" approach of bringing people to Sunday School from great distances.

The fellowship is ultraconservative in politics and revivalist in evangelism. They are militant champions of separation of church and state and are involved in promoting pressure to keep government control away from church work. Another area of adamant opposition is social ills such as dancing, drinking, smoking, gambling, movies and sexual immorality.

1966—NEW TESTAMENT ASSOCIATION OF INDEPENDENT BAPTIST CHURCHES

During the 1960s, a group of pastors and laymen within the Conservative Baptist Association became concerned with the trends they saw in the association. They felt that some were fostering or supporting ecumenism, were leaving the stated position on separation and were being involved with mass evangelism activities such as the Billy Graham Crusade.

There were twenty-seven churches participating in the organization in 1966, although over one hundred churches had participated in the formative stages during the two previous years. The association has churches in most midwestern states and some in the plain states. It has some relationship with two colleges and one seminary. Although there are few churches, most of which are relatively small, the churches have a growing number of Christian day schools in operation.

The association has more than fifty churches in fellowship at this time. Member churches are expected to participate personally and financially.

1978—EVANGELICAL FREE BAPTIST CHURCH

These twenty-two churches separated from the Southern Baptist Convention over a doctrinal dispute. Each church is sovereign, but the churches work cooperatively in institutional chaplaincies, personal problem hotlines and coffeehouse ministries. They support some missionary work in Mexico.

We have just looked at a representative sample of the divisions among Baptists in America, and we have noticed that the divisions are often based on doctrinal as well as practical differences. Often the differences are in peripheral rather than major theological areas.

While Baptists have tended to divide associationally, there have been a few attempts to bring many branches of Baptists together for cooperative fellowship. The Southern Baptists, for example, are quite tolerant of differing views, so that there are many varieties of Baptist practices within their major framework. Another attempt was the Baptist World Alliance, an international fellowship of mostly ecumenical Baptists, whose goal was to create a world consciousness of Baptists. Alliance sessions were held on an irregular basis in America and Europe. A third example is the Fundamental Baptist Congress, which came about in the 1960s to promote separatist Baptist positions by holding a large preaching conference every three years in different locations. No organizational connections were included to bind the participants together.

The history of Baptist associations demonstrates an emphasis on individuality and local sovereignty. Each association has some area of uniqueness in practice and, in some cases, doctrine. Such diversity makes each church an interesting historical study in itself.

5
The Baptist Use of Confessions of Faith

I believe in God the Father Almighty; and in Jesus Christ, His only begotten Son, our Lord, who was born of the Holy Spirit and the Virgin Mary, crucified under Pontius Pilate and buried; the third day He rose from the dead, ascended into the heavens, being seated at the right hand of the Father, whence He shall come to judge the living and the dead; and in the Holy Spirit, holy church, forgiveness of sins, resurrection of the flesh.
—the most ancient form
of the Apostles' Creed

Confessions of personal belief or of a collective group standard are common throughout the history of the church. Sometimes these confessions were given other names: Rule of Faith, Rule of the Church, some specific Creed, Articles of Faith, Standards, Symbols or Doctrinal Statement. Whatever the identifying name, a confession is designed to set forth the acceptable beliefs regarding interpretation of Scripture by a specific group of people.

Some church historians point out certain summary passages in the Gospels that are somewhat creedal in appearance. These historians suggest that statements made directly by God set out basic truths for belief statements:

At Jesus' baptism:

73

... This is my beloved Son, in whom I am well
pleased (Matt. 3:17).

At Jesus' transfiguration:

... This is my beloved Son, in whom I am well
pleased; hear ye him (Matt. 17:5).

At Jesus' prayer that He might glorify the Father's name in His
public ministry with the Gentile world:

I have both glorified it, and will glorify it again (John
12:28b).

John the Baptist made a very strong confession before a
large group of listeners that can be considered a summary of
great truth:

... Behold the Lamb of God, which taketh away the
sin of the world (John 1:29).

Peter offered a statement of truth when Jesus asked the
disciples who the people were saying He was. After the men
had reported the various responses, Jesus asked for an indica-
tion of their belief about Him, and Peter responded:

... Thou art the Christ, the Son of the living God
(Matt. 16:16).

Jesus connected faith, baptism, fellowship and instruction
for continuing the propagation of the gospel when He addressed His disciples after His resurrection:

Go ye therefore, and teach all nations, baptizing
them in the name of the Father, and of the Son, and
of the Holy Ghost: Teaching them to observe all
things whatsoever I have commanded you: and, lo, I
am with you alway, even unto the end of the world.
Amen (Matt. 28:19, 20).

The last instance of a confessional statement in the Gospels
comes from the apostle John regarding his purpose in relating
some of Jesus' activities:

But these are written, that ye might believe that
Jesus is the Christ, the Son of God; and that believing ye might have life through his name (John 20:31).

Other church historians emphasize creedal or confessional
statements in the Epistles.

A summary statement about essential faith unto salvation:

That if thou shalt confess with thy mouth the Lord

Jesus, and shalt believe in thine heart that God hath
raised him from the dead, thou shalt be saved.

For with the heart man believeth unto righteousness; and with the mouth confession is made unto
salvation (Rom. 10:9, 10).

A summary statement of creedal form regarding the gospel:

For I delivered unto you first of all that which I also
received, how that Christ died for our sins according
to the scriptures;

And that he was buried, and that he rose again the
third day according to the scriptures (1 Cor. 15:3, 4).

Paul's second letter to Timothy contains a brief statement
encompassing the truth and authority of the Scriptures:

All scripture is given by inspiration of God, and is
profitable for doctrine, for reproof, for correction,
for instruction in righteousness;

That the man of God may be perfect, throughly
furnished unto all good works (2 Tim. 3:16, 17).

It is obvious that confession statements in the Epistles are
more complicated than the simple statements of the Gospels.
It might be argued that the statements of the Epistles include
men's additions, thereby leaving them open to question of
their authority and authenticity. This writing technique, however, is used again and again in Scripture. It is called the "Law
of Second Reference." Since the Holy Spirit is the Author of
the whole of Scripture, He chooses to give an initial, brief statement, then later returns to the subject giving greater detail. The
accounts of creation in Genesis 1 and 2 are a good example of
this concept in consecutive chapters.

After the apostles left the formative church scene, many interpretations of the Scriptures came into existence. The word
heresies keeps appearing on the pages of history. A heresy is
casually described as anything someone believes that is different from generally accepted truth. For the believer who ac-
cepts the Scripture in totality, a heresy is a belief in something
other than what is taught in the Bible.

It seems that as the church spread over the Mediterranean
world, and many people were presenting themselves for baptism, some sort of short form of Biblical, essential beliefs had

to be written. The first of these was the Apostles' Creed. The Apostles' Creed appeared in Rome about A.D. 340, so obviously it was not written by the apostles. Rather, it was an attempt by someone to summarize what was believed to be the position of the apostles. Any candidate for baptism had to assent to believing what the creed stated. Many churches at the present time use this creed as a convenient summary statement of their beliefs.

As the study of theology progressed, differing conclusions were reached regarding essential doctrines. Along with the continued diversity caused by division, there was confusion among people regarding each other's beliefs. When Baptists appeared as an organized body in the early seventeenth century, it was necessary to facilitate their witness and their anti-Catholic position by preparing a statement of belief in a brief form. Actually, all creeds or confessions are drawn from the Bible, but they reflect different interpretations of Biblical essentials. The Baptist confessions vary from time to time as they also reflect differences in Biblical interpretation. They also move from simple to quite complex as the lines of difference become more distinct.

Several purposes are served by such confessions. First, they are aimed at maintaining purity of doctrine. An applicant for membership must acknowledge belief in the specific statements; thereby the nonconformer is kept from joining the fellowship. Second, the confessions clarify the Baptist position to those interested by including Bible verses for support. Third, the confessions provide guidelines to an association for counsel in theological disputes in the local churches. In Baptist organizational structure the confessions also provide for a check by the local churches regarding the maintenance of doctrinal purity by those in leadership. Fourth, the confessions serve as an aide to the indoctrination of the youth within the churches. Although not commonly used today, Baptists have had catechismal classes for instructional purposes. Published Baptist catechisms have been developed based upon a confession or doctrinal statement. And fifth, Baptists have often used confessions as guides for discipline. During the various forms of inquisitions in Europe and America, lack of adherence to some church confessions brought bodily punishment, imprisonment and, in many cases, death. Baptists, believing in freedom of religious expression, did not seek to force their faith upon unwilling subjects. Rather, they chose to discipline by withdrawing fellowship (or membership) from the person. Discipline thus preserved the individual's freedom of religious belief and practice while at the same time helping to maintain the doctrinal purity of the church. When applied to churches within associations, it served a similar purpose on a larger scale.

Hiscox's New Directory for Baptist Churches has a classic statement regarding Baptist confessions:

> Among American Baptists are to be found great numbers of formularies (confessions), in a great variety of expression, as the churches which use them, or the pastors who constructed them may be inclined, but with a remarkable—it may be said, with a marvelous—harmony of doctrinal statements.[1]

Certainly this reflects the individuality and the autonomy of local churches as they define themselves indigenously. What needs to be positively stated or defended differs from place to place and time to time, and yet there runs throughout each a mainstream of basic interpretation of Scripture.

Probably the earliest of Baptist confessions is the Short Confession of Faith in XX Articles by John Smyth (1609). Smyth had been a part of the Separatists in England, had migrated to Amsterdam, fellowshiped with the Mennonite branch of the Anabaptists and finally became a convinced Baptist. It is not surprising to find this very outspoken man publishing his views. Lumpkin published the text of this confession (Baptist Confessions of Faith [2]) as follows:

We believe with the heart and with the mouth confess:
(1) That there is one God, the best, the highest, and most

---

1. Hiscox, New Directory, 536.
2. William L. Lumpkin, Baptist Confessions of Faith (Valley Forge, PA: Judson Press, 1969), 100-101.

glorious Creator and Preserver of all; Who is Father, Son and
Holy Spirit;

(2) That God has created and redeemed the human race to
His own image and has ordained all men (no one being
reprobated) to life;

(3) That God imposes no necessity of sinning on anyone;
but man freely, by Satanic instigation, departs from God;

(4) That the law of life was originally placed by God in the
keeping of the law; then, by reason of the weakness of the
flesh, was, by the good pleasure of God, through the redemption of Christ, changed into justification of faith; on which account, no one ought justly to blame God, but rather, with his
inmost heart, to revere, adore and praise His mercy, that God
should have rendered that possible to man, by His grace,
which before, since man had fallen, was impossible by nature;

(5) That there is no original sin (lit., no sin of origin or descent), but all sin is actual and voluntary viz., a word, a deed or
a design against the law of God; and therefore, infants are
without sin;

(6) That Jesus Christ is true God and true Man; viz., the Son
of God taking to Himself, in addition, the true and pure nature
of a man, out of a true rational soul, and existing in a true
human body;

(7) That Jesus Christ, as pertaining to the flesh, was con-
ceived by the Holy Spirit in the womb of the Virgin Mary, after-
wards was born, circumcised, baptized, tempted; also that He
hungered, thirsted, ate, drank, increased both in stature and in
knowledge; He was wearied, He slept, at last was crucified,
dead, buried, He rose again, ascended into Heaven; and that
to Himself as only King, Priest, and Prophet of the church, all
power both in Heaven and earth is given;

(8) That the grace of God, through the finished redemption
of Christ, was to be prepared and offered to all without distinction, and that not feignedly but in good faith, partly by things
made, which declare the invisible things of God, and partly by
the preaching of the gospel;

(9) That men, of the grace of God through the redemption
of Christ, are able (the Holy Spirit, by grace, being before unto
them *grace prevenient*) to repent, to believe, to turn to God, and

to attain to eternal life; so on the other hand, they are able themselves to resist the Holy Spirit, to depart from God, and to perish forever;

(10) That the justification of man before the Divine tribunal (which is both the throne of justice and of mercy), consists partly of the imputation of the righteousness of Christ apprehended by faith, and partly of inherent righteousness, in the holy themselves, by the operation of the Holy Spirit, which is called regeneration or sanctification; since any one is righteous, who doeth righteousness;

(11) That faith, destitute of good works, is vain; but true and living faith is distinguished by good works;

(12) That the church of Christ is a company of the faithful, baptized after confession of sin and of faith, endowed with the power of Christ;

(13) That the church of Christ has power delegated to themselves of announcing the word, administering the sacraments, appointing ministers, disclaiming them, and also excommunicating; but the last appeal is to the brethren or body of the church;

(14) That baptism is the external sign of the remission of sins, of dying and being made alive, and therefore does not belong to infants;

(15) That the Lord's Supper is the external sign of the communion of Christ, and the faithful amongst themselves by faith and love;

(16) That the ministers of the church are, not only bishops (episcopos), to whom the power is given of dispensing both the word and the sacraments, but also deacons, men and widows, who attend to the affairs of the poor and sick brethren;

(17) That brethren who persevere in sins known to themselves, after the third admonition, are to be excluded from the fellowship of the saints by excommunication;

(18) That those who are excommunicated are not to be avoided in what pertains to worldly business (civile commercium);

(19) That the dead (the living being instantly changed) will rise again with the same bodies; not the substance, but the qualities being changed;

(20) That after the resurrection, all will be borne to the

tribunal of Christ, the Judge, to be judged according to their works; the pious, after sentence of absolution, will enjoy eternal life with Christ in Heaven; the wicked, condemned, will be punished with eternal torments in hell with the devil and his angels.

Other confessions followed: A *Short Confession of Faith* (1610); A *Declaration of Faith of English People Remaining at Amsterdam* (1611) and *Propositions and Conclusions Concerning True Christian Religion* (1612-14). Each of these reflected special concerns, mostly relating to association with the Mennonites in Holland.

In 1644, seven Particular Baptist churches in the London area met to form an association and wrote their own strongly Calvinistic confession. It was an opportune time for this first Baptist confession on British soil to be produced. The power of the Crown had been partially destroyed, parliamentary government was becoming a reality, ecclesiastical tyranny had been broken, and for the moment religious freedom allowed preachers to move about the communities in promotion of evangelism. The Baptists were especially active and, as is true of many growing organizations, soon met opposition which linked them with radicalism much like that of the Anabaptists on the Continent. The London Confession of 1644, therefore, is an attempt to proclaim what the Baptists believed while at the same time defending against the charges of the enemy.

Several other specific confessions were written in propagation or defense during the next thirty years, but most of these reflected local issues. Each confession championed religious liberty and countered the linking of the Baptists with the radical Anabaptist movement.

In 1688, pastors and messengers of about one hundred churches in Wales and England authorized the formation of a new confession. Several additional statements, or "chapters," were added to the London Confession of 1644, and the whole thing was rearranged in the order of the Westminster Confession which had been drawn up by the Church of England (1643-1647). The document was signed in September 1689 by thirty-seven ministers. Of special interest are the additional "chapters" dealing with the obligation to preach the gospel to all nations at all times; the importance of singing hymns and "spiritual songs"; the disuse of the term "sacrament" and a provision allowing for lay preachers. To save costs, the printers simply updated copies of a confession of faith printed in 1677. Hence, the Second London Confession of 1689 has the date 1677 on its title page. The table of contents reads:

Chapter
1. Of the Holy Scriptures
2. Of God and the Trinity
3. Of God's Decrees
4. Of Creation
5. Of Divine Providence
6. Of the Fall of Man, of Sin, and the Punishment thereof
7. Of God's Covenant
8. Of Christ the Mediator
9. Of Free Will
10. Of Effectual Calling
11. Of Justification
12. Of Adoption
13. Of Sanctification
14. Of Saving Faith
15. Of Repentance unto Life and Salvation
16. Of Good Works
17. Of Perseverance of Saints
18. Of the Assurance of Grace and Salvation
19. Of the Law of God
20. Of the Gospel, and the extent of the Grace thereof
21. Of Christian Liberty and the Liberty of Conscience
22. Of Religious Worship, and the Sabbath Day
23. Of Lawful Oaths and Vows
24. Of the Civil Magistrate
25. Of Marriage
26. Of the Church
27. Of the Communion of Saints
28. Of Baptism and the Lord's Supper
29. Of Baptism
30. Of the Lord's Supper
31. Of the State of Man after death, and the Resurrection of the dead

32. Of the Last Judgment

An Appendix concerning Baptism

This format has served as the model for most of the confessions written since that time.

The Second London Confession was used by most Baptists in America after 1689, but no copies were printed here. The Philadelphia Association changed the statement only briefly by adding a section that made ordinances of singing in worship services and the laying on of hands at baptism. They also added an appendix on discipline. So in 1742 the Philadelphia Confession of Faith was printed with thirty-four articles or chapters. Later publications dropped the additions and made it essentially the same as the Second London Confession.

Of special importance is the formation of the New Hampshire Confession. Hiscox indicates that there is a great deal of confusion about its origin.[3] Lumpkin, however, finds the formation of this confession to have been in 1830 by the authority of the Baptist Convention of New Hampshire.[4] The necessity for this new statement of belief may have been occasioned by the rise of the Freewill Baptists in the area. As a result, the New Hampshire Confession states its Calvinism very moderately rather than in the extreme stances of earlier confessions. Apparently there are no copies of the original New Hampshire Confession available today, but the lengthy statement with Scripture references can be found in Hiscox's *New Directory for Baptist Churches*, pages 543 through 563, and another without Scripture references in Lumpkin's *Baptist Confessions of Faith*, pages 360 through 367.

Adaptations of the New Hampshire Confession have been made, usually by adding detail, and adopted by numerous Baptist associations in America. In 1925, the Southern Baptist Convention made about ten changes in the New Hampshire Confession and adopted it as an expression of their generally accepted views. Earlier, the Landmark Baptists had accepted the confession with few modifications, and the American Baptist Association had done the same in 1902.

3. Hiscox, 543-563.
4. Lumpkin, 360-367.

Interestingly, the Northern Baptist Convention chose not to issue any doctrinal statement at its founding in 1907. This organization (now the American Baptist Churches) continues to operate on the idea that such creeds or confessions are not baptistic because the Bible in itself is a sufficient statement of faith. This idea allows for the wide range of doctrinal and theological interpretations within the denomination.

During the 1920s, the Baptist Bible Union of America was formed within the Northern Baptist Convention to rid the missionaries and the educational institutions of heresy. In an effort to clearly state their position, the union, under the leadership of several fundamentalist men, framed its own eighteen articles of faith:

    I. Of the Scriptures
   II. Of the True God
  III. Of the Holy Spirit
   IV. Of the Devil or Satan
    V. Of the Creation
   VI. Of the Fall of Man
  VII. Of the Virgin Birth
 VIII. Of the Atonement for Sin
   IX. Of Grace in the New Creation
    X. Of the Freeness of Salvation
   XI. Of Justification
  XII. Of Repentance and Faith
 XIII. Of the Church
  XIV. Of Baptism and the Lord's Supper
   XV. Of the Perseverance of the Saints
  XVI. Of the Righteous and the Wicked
 XVII. Of Civil Government
XVIII. Of the Resurrection, Return of Christ and Related
       Events

When the General Association of Regular Baptist Churches was begun by those withdrawing from the Northern Baptist Convention, they accepted the New Hampshire Confession with some modifications. The most notable change related to a clearer, definitive statement on the doctrine of eschatology, or Last Things. The association, formed in 1932, adopted the following confession of faith in 1933. The account used here does not reflect any modifications adopted by the association since its inception, but it does show that the confession is closely related to the New Hampshire Confession.

Confession of Faith

I. Of the Scriptures (very close to the New Hampshire, Article I)

We believe that the Holy Bible as originally written was verbally inspired and the product of Spirit-controlled men, and therefore has truth without any admixture of error for its matter. We believe the Bible to be the true center of Christian union and the supreme standard by which all human conduct, creeds and opinions shall be tried.

2 Tim. 3:16, 17; 2 Pet. 1:19-21

II. Of the True God (very close to the New Hampshire, Article II)

We believe there is one, and only one, living and true God, and infinite, intelligent Spirit, and Maker and Supreme Ruler of Heaven and earth; inexpressibly glorious in holiness, and worthy of all possible honor, confidence and love; that in the unity of the Godhead there are three Persons, the Father, the Son and the Holy Ghost, equal in every divine perfection, and executing distinct but harmonious offices in the great work of redemption.

Exod. 20:2, 3; 1 Cor. 8:6; 1 John 5:7; Rev. 4:11

III. Of the Holy Spirit (no specific statement in the New Hampshire)

We believe that the Holy Spirit is a divine Person; equal with God the Father and God the Son and of the same nature; that He was active in the Creation; that in His relation to the unbelieving world He restrains the Evil One until God's purpose is fulfilled; that He convicts of sin, of righteousness, and of judgment; that He bears witness to the truth of the gospel in preaching and testimony; that He is the agent of the New Birth; that He seals, baptizes, endues, guides, teaches, witnesses, sanctifies and helps the believer.

Gen. 1:1-3; Matt. 28:19; Mark 1:8; Luke 1:35; 24:49; John 1:33; 3:5, 6; 14:16, 17; 14:26; 16:8-11; Acts 5:30-32; 11:16; Rom. 8:14, 16, 26, 27; Eph. 1:13, 14; Heb. 9:14

IV. Of the Devil, or Satan (no specific statement in the
     New Hampshire)
We believe in the personality of Satan, that he is the unholy god of this age, and the author of all the powers of darkness, and is destined to the judgment of an eternal justice in the Lake of Fire.
Matt. 4:1-3; 2 Cor. 4:4; Rev. 20:10

V. Of the Creation (no specific statement in the
    New Hampshire)
We accept the Genesis account of creation and believe that man came by direct creation of God and not by evolution.
Gen. 1; 2; Col. 1:16, 17; John 1:3

VI. Of the Fall of Man (close to the New Hampshire,
     Article III)
We believe that man was created in innocence under the law of his Maker, but by voluntary transgression fell from his sinless and happy state in consequence of which all mankind are now sinners, not only by constraint, but of choice, and therefore under just condemnation without defense or excuse.
Gen. 3:1-6, 24; Rom. 1:18, 32; 3:10-19; 5:12, 19

VII. Of the Virgin Birth (no specific statement in the
      New Hampshire)
We believe that Jesus Christ was begotten of the Holy Ghost in a miraculous manner; born of Mary, a virgin, as no other man was ever born or can ever be born of woman, and that He is both the Son of God and God, the Son.
Gen. 3:15; Isa. 7:14; Matt. 1:18-25; Luke 1:35; John 1:14

VIII. Of the Atonement for Sin (very close to the
       New Hampshire, Article IV)
We believe that the salvation of sinners is wholly of grace; through the mediatorial offices of the Son of God, Who by the

appointment of the Father, freely took upon Him our nature, yet without sin, honored the divine law by His personal obedience, and by His death made a full and vicarious atonement for our sins; that His atonement consisted not in setting us an example by His death as a martyr, but was a voluntary substitution of Himself in the sinner's place, the just dying for the unjust; Christ, the Lord, bearing our sins in His own body on the tree; that having risen from the dead, He is now enthroned in Heaven, and uniting in His wonderful Person the tenderest sympathies with divine perfection, He is in every way qualified to be a suitable, a compassionate, and an all-sufficient Savior.

Isa. 53:4-7; Matt. 18:11; John 3:16; Acts 15:11; Rom. 3:24, 25; 1 Cor. 15:3; 2 Cor. 5:21; Eph. 2:8; Phil. 2:7; Heb. 2:14; 1 John 4:10

IX. Of Grace in the New Creation (this is a combination of statements in the New Hampshire, Articles VII and IX)

We believe that in order to be saved, sinners must be born again; that the new birth is a new creation in Christ Jesus; that it is instantaneous and not a process; that in the New Birth the one dead in trespasses and in sins is made a partaker of the divine nature and receives eternal life, the free gift of God; that the new creation is brought about in a manner above our comprehension, solely by the power of the Holy Spirit in connection with divine truth, so as to secure our voluntary obedience to the gospel; that its proper evidence appears in the holy fruits of repentance and faith and newness of life.

John 3:3, 6-8; Acts 16:30-33; Rom. 6:23; 2 Cor. 5:17, 19; Eph. 2:1; Col. 2:13; 2 Pet. 1:4; 1 John 5:1

X. Of Justification (very close to the New Hampshire, Article V)

We believe that the great gospel blessing which Christ secures to such as believe in Him is justification;

(a) That justification includes the pardon of sin, and the gift of eternal life on principles of righteousness;

(b) That it is bestowed not in consideration of any works of righteousness which we have done; but solely through faith in

the Redeemer's blood, His righteousness is imputed to us.
Isa. 53:11; Zech. 13:1; Acts 13:39; Rom. 5:1, 9; 8:1

XI. Of Faith and Salvation (completely different wording,
but similar in essence to the New Hampshire, Article
VIII)

We believe that faith in the Lord Jesus Christ is the only
condition of salvation.
Acts 16:31

XII. Of the Local Church (the first third of this statement is
all that the New Hampshire, Article XIII contains)

We believe that a local church is a congregation of immersed believers, associated by covenant of faith and
fellowship of the gospel; observing the ordinances of Christ;
governed by His laws; and exercising the gifts, rights and
privileges invested in them by His Word; that its officers are
pastors and deacons, whose qualifications, claims and duties
are clearly defined in the Scriptures; we believe the true mission of the church is the faithful witnessing of Christ to all men
as we have opportunity. We hold that the local church has the
absolute right of self-government, free from the interference of
any hierarchy of individuals or organizations; and that the one
and only true superintendent is Christ, through the Holy Spirit;
that it is Scriptural for true churches to cooperate with each
other in contending for the faith and for the furtherance of the
gospel; that every church is the sole judge of the measure and
method of its cooperation; on all matters of membership, of
polity, of government, of discipline, of benevolence, the will of
the local church is final.
Acts 2:41, 42; 15:13-18; 20:17-28; 1 Cor. 11:2; Eph. 1:22,
23; 4:11; 5:23-32; Col. 1:18; 1 Tim. 3

XIII. Of Baptism and the Lord's Supper (a very close
statement to the New Hampshire, Article XIV)

We believe that Christian baptism is the immersion of a
believer in water to show forth in a solemn and beautiful
emblem of faith in the crucified, buried and risen Savior, with
its effect in our death to sin and resurrection to a new life; that

it is a prerequisite to the privileges of a church relation. We believe that the Lord's Supper is the commemoration of His death until He come, and should be preceded always by solemn self-examination.

Matt. 3:16; John 3:23; Acts 8:36-39; Rom. 6:3-5; 1 Cor. 11:23-28; Col. 2:12

XIV. Of the Security of the Saints (very close, but much shorter than the New Hampshire, Article XI)

We believe that those who are truly born again are kept by God the Father for Jesus Christ.

John 10:28, 29; Rom. 8:35-39; Phil. 1:6; Jude 1

XV. Of the Righteous and the Wicked (close to the New Hampshire, Article XVII)

We believe that there is a radical and essential difference between the righteous and the wicked; that such only as through faith are justified in the name of the Lord Jesus Christ, and sanctified by the Spirit of our God, are truly righteous in His esteem; while all such as continue in impenitence and unbelief are in His sight wicked, and under the curse; and this distinction holds among men both in and after death, in the everlasting felicity of the saved and the everlasting conscious suffering of the lost.

Gen. 18:23; Prov. 14:32; Mal. 3:18; Matt. 25:34-41; Luke 6:25; John 8:21; Rom. 6:17, 18, 23; 7:6; 1 John 5:19

XVI. Of Civil Government (exactly the same as the New Hampshire, Article XVI)

We believe that civil government is of divine appointment, for the interests and good order of human society; that magistrates are to be prayed for, conscientiously honored and obeyed; except in things opposed to the will of our Lord Jesus Christ Who is the only Lord of the conscience, and the coming Prince of the kings of the earth.

Exod. 18:21, 22; 2 Sam. 23:3; Dan. 3:17, 18; Matt. 22:21; Acts 4:19, 20; 5:29; 23:5; Rom. 13:1-7

XVII. Of the Resurrection, Personal, Visible, Premillenial
    Return of Christ, the Related Events (this is a much
    more detailed and very different style of statement
    than the New Hampshire, Article XVIII)
(a) We believe in the Bodily Resurrection
Matt. 28:6, 7; Mark 16:6; Luke 24:2-6, 39; John 20:27;
1 Cor. 15:4
(b) The Ascension
Mark 16:19; Luke 24:51; Acts 1:9-11; Heb. 12:2; Rev. 3:21
(c) The High Priesthood
1 Tim. 2:5; Heb. 2:17; 5:9, 10; 8:6; 1 John 2:1
(d) The Second Coming
John 14:3; Acts 1:11; 1 Thess. 4:16; Heb. 9:28; James 5:8
(e) The Resurrection of the Righteous Dead
1 Cor. 15:42-44, 52; 1 Thess. 4:13-18
(f) The Change of the Living in Christ
1 Cor. 15:51-53; Phil. 3:20, 21; 1 Thess. 4:13-18
(g) The Throne of David
Isa. 9:6, 7; Luke 1:32; Acts 2:29, 30
(h) The Millennial Reign
Ps. 72:8; Isa. 11:4, 5; 32:1; 1 Cor. 15:25; Rev. 20:6, 14

(The above contrast is made by using a copy of the New
Hampshire Confession as found in Lumpkin's *Baptist Confessions
of Faith* and a copy of the Confession of Faith of the General
Association of Regular Baptist Churches as found in Stowell's
*The General Association of Regular Baptist Churches: Background and
History*.)
    The New Hampshire Confession includes statements or ar-
ticles entitled "Of the Freedom of Salvation," "Of the Harmony
of the Law and the Gospel" and "Of the Christian Sabbath"
that are not in the above articles at all. In 1853, two additional
articles were added to the New Hampshire Confession, "Of
Repentance and Faith" and "Of Sanctification." These articles
reflected some of the newer problems faced by Baptists at that
time.
    The same thing happened with the Confession of Faith of
the General Association of Regular Baptist Churches. From
time to time pressure was applied to clarify and more

adequately confront new and different beliefs that needed attention. Articles on salvation, sanctification, separation and Israel were added. The entire confession was reworded and rearranged with approval by the association at the annual meetings in 1975 and 1976.

The development of confessions tends to move from the simple statement issued at the beginning or founding of the movement to an increasingly detailed and definitive series of statements. Perhaps this pattern indicates that as movements grow chronologically older, they feel they must take more drastic measures to ensure compliance and minimize defection. Unfortunately, they do not seem to realize that those same measures carry in them the seeds of destruction of the movement itself. Regardless of the reasons and potential dangers, it is very apparent that changes and refinements do become necessary from time to time. Therefore, no universal, enduring, standard confession could be developed satisfactory to any large segment of Baptist churches.

6
Baptist Expansion Among the British (1600-1900)

I have taken a deep interest in the struggles of the orthodox brethren, but I have never advised those struggles, nor entertained the slightest hope of their success. My course has been of another kind. As soon as I saw, or thought I saw, that error had become firmly established, I did not deliberate, but quitted the body at once. Since then my counsel has been "come out from among them." I have felt that no protest could be equal to that of distinct separation.

—Charles Haddon Spurgeon

As one reads through the accounts of Baptist development and expansion in Britain, a classic study of the independence, autonomy and indigenous principles treasured by Baptists stands out clearly. John Smyth established the Baptist position while a part of the Separatist exile in Amsterdam. Thomas Helwys elaborated on these early formulations and brought them back to England sometime around 1612. From these men's work came the Baptist movement in Britain.

Smyth died without returning to his native England, but Helwys returned to London and began the first Baptist church in England. The theology of this group was Arminian, as would be expected because of their close ties with the Anabaptist Mennonites in Holland. Henry Vedder, in his *Short History of the*

Baptists, mentions that the Baptists in England and the Mennonites in Holland had a close relationship.[1] They apparently exchanged members freely and without question. It is even reported that when the early Baptist groups had internal conflicts they sought arbitration from the Mennonites. There might be cause for concern about the method and mode of baptism among the early Baptists, because the Mennonites practiced what was called aspersion, or sprinkling. However, while there may have been considerable discussion about sprinkling in the very earliest days, it is certain that the British Baptists had adopted immersion by the middle of the sixteenth century because their fellowship with the Mennonites was broken. Vedder suggests that the only logical explanation for this break comes from the Mennonite writers who indicate that "the adoption of immersion by the English churches . . . practically pronounced the Mennonite brethren unbaptized."[2] From about 1650 onward, there is no evidence that Baptists practiced sprinkling of believers but instead continually practiced immersion.

The early Baptists of the strain begun by Helwys, John Murton and others soon were given the name General Baptists. The name is descriptive: *General*, they accepted a general atonement for all men; *Baptist*, they practiced only believer's immersion.

By 1626 another group of Baptists appeared in the religious world of the British. Five churches with a total membership of no more than 150 had taken a different position. Later they became known as Particular Baptists. Again the name is descriptive: *Particular*, they held to a particular atonement effective only for the elect; *Baptist*, they practiced only believer's immersion. As the British became more tolerant of other religions, both General and Particular Baptist groups preached and taught New Testament truth effectively, and there was the accompanying increase in the number of churches in both groups.

1. Henry C. Vedder, A *Short History of the Baptists* (Philadelphia: the American Baptist Publication Society, 1907), 209.
2. Ibid.

Knowing that the General Baptists grew out of the Helwys background, it is important to look at the beginning of the Particular Baptists. Evidence is not very conclusive in any direction, but the consensus of most Baptist historians is that the Particular Baptists began under the leadership of Henry Jacob in London in 1616. In 1622, Jacob resigned his church and came to Virginia where he died in 1624. His successor in London was John Lathrop who later fled from the persecution by Archbishop Laud, coming to New England for safety.

Expansion and growth of the Baptist groups would have been much more rapid had they not fallen into theological controversy. There had been the difference between General and Particular Baptists regarding the atonement, but this had not been a problem within any one church. Within Jacob's church the question of baptism caused a serious rift. Lathrop apparently was not convinced about immersion, and there was debate over which churches had authority to conduct the ordinance. It appears that they continued immersion, and the conflict produced further separation—seventeen members left, according to Vedder, and later another six joined them in a church pastored by John Spilsbury.[3]

The Jacob church divided in 1640 with Mr. Jessey giving leadership to one group and Mr. Barebone giving leadership to the other. Vedder quotes a lengthy section from the records of the church at that time with the exact spellings, a portion of which says:

> The Church became two by mutuall consent just half being with Mr. P. Barebone, and ye other halfe with Mr. H. Jessey. Mr. Richd Blunt with him being convinced of Baptism yt also it ought to be by dipping in ye Body into ye Water, resembling Burial and riseing again. . .[4]

From that time forward there was little question regarding the form of believer's baptism among the Baptists until the entrance of liberal teaching in the late nineteenth century.

The question of which churches had authority to baptize

3. Vedder, 206.
4. Ibid., 207.

people was also settled about that same time. The Roman church and the Anglican church claimed the necessity of an uninterrupted succession of authorized persons (beginning with the apostles) to administer what they called the sacraments. Vedder quotes Thomas Crosby, an early Baptist historian, on the matter:

> But the greatest number of the English Baptists looked upon ... what proceeded from the old popish doctrine of right to administer the sacraments by an uninterrupted succession, which neither the Church of Rome nor the Church of England, much less the modern dissenters, could prove to be with them. They affirmed, therefore, and practiced accordingly, that after a general corruption of baptism, an unbaptized person might warrantably baptize, and so begin a reformation.[5]

This controversy, then, was closed also and was not revived for further debate among the Particular Baptists, but there does not seem to be any conclusive evidence either of conflict or resolution among the General Baptists. It can only be assumed that they practiced a similar position.

With all this internal conflict and slow growth, the Baptists also had to contend with political resistance. When Oliver Cromwell rose to prominence in England, the Baptists were certain that they had found a friend in high political office. Baptists, ever the champions of religious liberty, stood strong with the parliamentary side against the power of the Crown. Many Baptist men joined the army, and with military experience came the usual reward of political appointment and trust.

Some Baptists, like John and Henry Denne and Vavasor Powell, became active in politics, but their activity became somewhat radical. In fact, Cromwell at one point had John Denne imprisoned and his district declared a Protectorate. Cromwell's action threatened religious liberty, and many preachers spoke out against this severe abuse of power. Cromwell began to discharge many of the Baptists in his army and increased his power even further.

5. Ibid., 207-208.

As is true in most times of frustration, a group of radical Baptists rose to exert influence. These radicals became known as Fifth Monarchy Men and were led by some ex-soldiers discharged from service by Cromwell. Essentially they espoused the idea of establishing the Fifth Kingdom of Daniel by force. Armed to overthrow the King of England in 1661, they began an uprising that completely failed. The Fifth Monarchy movement itself failed, and with it came the discrediting of many Baptists because of their association with these radicals. Systematically the British government sought to reduce the freedom of religious expression for all except the established Church of England. The Five Mile Act in 1665 forbade the "nonconforming" (to the state church) to preach, teach or conduct religious services within five miles of any town. Violators were imprisoned. Declarations of toleration or indulgence were passed in 1672 and 1687 which temporarily ended the persecutions.

During this time of extreme difficulty, the Baptist movement continued to grow. This growth was made evident by a ten thousand member increase among General Baptists between 1660 and 1688. The more Calvinistic Particular Baptists experienced a slower rate of growth. After the Act of Toleration was passed in 1687, the opportunity was there for significant evangelization and growth, but the Baptists' zeal did not begin to match the opportunity.

Theological differences again demanded time and energy, detracting from a strong gospel advance during the eighteenth century. Arianism, which taught that Jesus was not fully God, was accepted in a measure by the more rationalistic leaders among Baptists. Hyper-Calvinism was accepted by many who were more closely influenced by reformed theology. Torbet demonstrates the fragmentation:

> The extent of doctrinal variation among English Baptists may be illustrated by a classification of ministers of London in 1731, which was as follows: seven antinomian or hyper-Calvinist, seven Calvinist, six Arminian, three Unitarian, and two Seventh-Day.[6]

6. Robert G. Torbet, A *History of the Baptists* (Valley Forge, PA: Judson Press, 1969), 63.

This number of differences reflects the independence of Baptists, but they were affected indigenously as well. The first half of the eighteenth century saw England in a state of change. New constitutional policies were being implemented, the first industrial revolution was underway, and societal life was becoming more complex and required greater organizational structure. As a result, the local churches were undergoing change as well, and these adjustments deterred their involvement in outreach.

The Church of England was becoming increasingly more corrupt and immoral, being influenced early by a venal King Charles II. The decline persisted even after his death in 1685. Vedder quotes Bishop Ryle on the deplorable condition of the established church in England:

> From the year 1700 till about the era of the French Revolution, England seemed barren of all good. . . . There was darkness in high places and darkness in low places; darkness in the court, the camp, the Parliament, and the bar; darkness in the country and darkness in town; darkness among rich, and darkness among poor—a gross, thick, religious and moral darkness; a darkness that might be felt.[7]

The clergy of the established church are depicted in literature as drunken, lustful, gambling, swearing and unfaithful. The church had taken its cue from the behavior of the political leadership. Instead of remaining true to the Scriptures, the church adopted rationalism to justify its behavior. The preachers were timid, apologizing for their "faith," and, of course, preached what would be called in the 1970s and 1980s a relative ethic.

The Baptist witness, while not caught up in the contemporary turning away from the Scriptures, was certainly affected by it. In such times of difficulty, however, God always seems to raise up a man who encourages, challenges and inspires in a right direction. A young Oxford University student, committed to the Church of England, was sent on a mission to America. In Georgia he met some Moravians who shared with him for the

7. Vedder, 243.

first time the true meaning of the gospel. The young man returned to England in 1738, and in a meeting of the Moravian Society in London, John Wesley trusted Christ alone for his salvation. England, thereafter, was shaken by the preaching of this man. The new birth he preached, and immediate justification by faith! George Whitefield, a fellow student at Oxford, had been saying these things before, but he was not as capable in leadership as Wesley. They joined a religious club given the nickname "Methodists" and together began a religious revival. A new religious zeal took hold of England—the Church of England was revived and for fifty years produced some great ministers. A new moral revival changed attitudes and policies regarding ethical issues, and skepticism decreased as religion became more respectable among the influential.

How did all this affect the Baptists? It opened the door for significant growth, zeal and ultimately missionary work. The General Baptists were the first to experience revival of spiritual interest. Not all Baptists, however, joined in the enthusiasm and so, consequently, under the leadership of a Wesleyan convert who became a convinced Baptist, the "New Connexion" Baptist Association was formed. Dan Taylor, its founder, became a catalyst for the movement. He was not formally educated but took advantage of many opportunities to develop his mind. He had boundless energy and seemed never to tire. He edited a magazine, preached any time he was needed, established a fund for educating young preachers, acted as principal of an academy (actually a seminary) and traveled up and down England proclaiming the gospel. Vedder eulogizes this man who died in his chair at age 78:

> God makes no mistakes; he never selects for a great
> work the lazy, half-hearted, weak-willed man, but
> one who has energy and grit and perseverance, as
> well as piety. It is impossible to bore through granite
> with a boiled carrot; it requires a steel drill.[8]

The change among the Particular Baptists, while less dramatic, was no less meaningful. The change was largely due to one of God's men, Andrew Fuller. He was deeply convicted

8. Ibid., 248.

of sin as a young boy but did not hear the way of salvation for several years. Once he did, he accepted the truth of the Scriptures and was born again. In 1770, at age sixteen, he witnessed for the first time a baptism by immersion and a month later was himself immersed. At age twenty-one he was ordained to the ministry and became the pastor of a church which he served until his death in 1815. He was not a great public speaker but was a sound and convincing preacher, writer, thinker and teacher. His materials were widely read and influenced the Particular Baptists toward a modified Calvinism. This acknowledgement that Christ's atoning sacrifice was sufficient for all who believe, but that they will only come as influenced by the Holy Spirit and the Word, became the basic belief of nearly all Baptists from that time forward. Thus, the distinctions between General and Particular Baptists were lost for the most part.

Fuller was not only interested in local church matters, he also became involved in the formation of a Baptist missionary society and traveled widely in its promotion. It is not surprising that as a result of this man's ministry, God selected a young man whose ministry would exceed the bounds of his fathers. He was born to a churchman of the state church who taught him a definite horror of all "dissenters," among which were the Baptists. William Carey, however, heard the gospel teaching under Pastor Fuller, accepted it, was baptized by Dr. John Ryland and became the founder of Baptist missions—in fact, *all* foreign missions. Little did Pastor Fuller know that this humble young journeyman in the shoe-making business would become great in the annals of Christian history.

Following in the path of all this enthusiastic gospel outreach, nearly seventeen hundred new Baptist churches were begun in England from 1800 to 1870. This in part was due to the formation of the Baptist Home Mission Society in 1779 and the Baptist Union in 1832. But increases do not come from good organization alone: there must be capable men to carry out the policies. The Baptists had two men of special ability.

One of these men was a precocious, remarkable child who became a remarkable man. Robert Hall was so sensitive that he could not speak aloud in his schooling without breaking down. He had read volumes on theology and mastered them by the time he was nine years old. In college, he knew the material but could not communicate—a serious deficiency for a preacher. He went to King's College, Aberdeen, Scotland, and there matured, overcoming his fears of public speaking. He became a pastor, serving successfully in three city congregations. His sermons were printed and widely read. His preaching was stately and sometimes cumbersome, but when he died in 1831, one of the great preachers of Baptist antiquity passed from the scene.

A man of very different background and character was born in 1834 and is the second of the great men of the Baptist pulpit in the nineteenth century. Better known generally among Baptists than Robert Hall is Charles Haddon Spurgeon. A Christian since the age of seventeen, he affiliated with the Baptist church and soon began to preach. He was a teacher in a private school, so he had what would be the equivalent of an American high school education. His preaching demands made it impossible for him to gain further formal training, but his success in the pulpit was sustained until his death in 1892. He held but one pastorate, the Southwark Baptist Church in London, from 1853 to 1892. Spurgeon, known the world over for his preaching, was also a builder: a church membership of over five thousand, a school (Pastor's College) for preparing ministers, an orphanage (Stockwell Orphanage) which cared for over five hundred children a year, a colportage association for literature distribution, a book fund to help preachers purchase books and a religious magazine (*The Sword and the Trowel*) for spiritual upbuilding of its readers. Spurgeon was a moderate Calvinist in theology and stood firmly against what he saw near the end of his life-ministry as a downward progression among the religions. Devoted to preaching the pure gospel of Christ, Spurgeon came into conflict with adherents of a lax religious practice within the Baptist ranks. He finally withdrew his fellowship from the Baptist Union in 1887. The kind of laxness he saw was comparable to what later would be called modernism, and still later, liberalism. Spurgeon refused to fellowship with liberals, or with those who were associated with liberals, but continued his great ministry of the gospel until his death.

Other famous preachers of the nineteenth century will be

mentioned only briefly. Alexander Maclaren (1825-1910), a very original and eloquent preacher from Scotland, was educated and ministered successfully in England. John Clifford (1836-1923), a scholarly and polished preacher and writer, influenced the whole cause of nonconformity in England. In some respects he was quite ecumenical because he served as president of the National Council of Evangelical Free Churches for a year or two and was the founder and president of the Baptist World Alliance from 1905 to 1911.

It must be remembered that the Baptists developed in England in a hostile environment where both state and state church sought to destroy its witness. Even the American revivalists found little success in England. The efforts of Moody and Torrey saw results, but they were not at all proportionate with population growth. A measure of spiritual compromise and decline, as seen by Spurgeon, soon became the more dominant force and the National Council of Evangelical Free Churches (composed of Baptists, Congregationalists, Presbyterians and Methodists) became the voice for Baptists in Britain. The local churches had voluntarily traded away certain limitations on their sovereignty in order to have a wider fellowship, which they believed would yield a more effective outreach ministry. These compromises led to attempts at amalgamation in local areas. Torbet reports thirty-five such experiments in London with only thirteen surviving until 1928. Of these thirteen, only three became thoroughly Baptist in theology and practice, two became Congregationalist, leaving only eight as union congregations.[9] He also points out that there are many Baptists in Britain today who do not consider believer's immersion important as a requirement for church membership.[10] By 1962 there were approximately three thousand Baptist churches in England, Scotland, Wales and Ireland, with a total membership of just over 300,000, according to The Baptist World.[11]

Baptist expansion apparently peaked among the British

9. Torbet, 129.
10. Ibid.
11. The Baptist World, June 1962.

about 1870. There followed a series of consolidation efforts which had less zeal and commitment. The result was a trend away from the historic distinctives of early Baptists and toward theological compromise and ecumenical practice, which obliterates the uniqueness that instills loyalty and aggressive evangelism.

7

Baptist Expansion in America to 1900

The Baptists say, and have always said, that the mercy of God and the grace of Jesus Christ are free and open to any man. They have been imprisoned for saying it, publicly whipped for saying it, driven into the wilderness, killed for saying it, and they have gone right on saying it, and they say it now: The mercy of God and the grace of Jesus Christ are free to any man. Knock and it shall be opened. God is always there Himself, waiting for each man to come in. The way is clear. You have access.

—Josef Nordenhaug

The story of the Baptists in America actually begins in England about 1600 with the birth of a boy named Roger Williams. Accounts differ regarding the year of birth. Childers says it was in the year that Queen Elizabeth died, which would make it 1603.[1] *The Baptist Encyclopedia* places his birth in 1599 and claims evidence that his baptism was on July 24, 1600.[2] Vedder uses Williams's birthdate as 1607.[3] Whatever the date

---

1. James S. Childers, ed., *The Way Home* (New York: Holt, Rinehart and Winston, 1964), 11.
2. Cathcart, *Baptist Encyclopedia*, 1250.
3. Vedder, *Short History*, 288.

of his birth, the beginning of the Baptist movement in America is marked by the arrival of Roger Williams in America.

Roger Williams was born the son of William Williams, a Welshman. Little is known about his early years, but apparently his religious views caused him some sorrow and persecution early in life. *The Baptist Encyclopedia* offers two quotations from Roger Williams:

> In 1673, Williams wrote: "From my childhood, now about threescore years, the Father of lights and mercies touched my soul with a love to himself, to his only begotten, the true Lord Jesus, and to his holy Scriptures."
>
> In 1632, Williams had written that he had been "persecuted in and out of my father's house these twenty years."[4]

Such statements underscore the idea that Roger Williams's view on the authority of Scripture as the only rule in religious matters was contrary to the state church and to the beliefs of his Anglican parents, who had had him baptized into the church while he was a baby. The beliefs of this young man made him a "nonconformist" and identified him with the Puritans, who were hated in England.

Somewhere in his early years, Williams learned a very new art called shorthand. Only a few knew this invention, and it brought him great opportunities. One of England's controversial lawyers, Sir Edward Coke, became interested in Williams and helped him through his schooling, including a time at Cambridge University. Coke had known of Thomas Helwys, who at one time had addressed the king of England in opposition to the belief in the divine right of kings to rule arbitrarily. At the time of his association with Williams, Coke was pressuring the king as Helwys had done, and King James was very angry about it. Coke, however, was too powerful a figure in London for the king to imprison as he had so many others. Perhaps in conversation Coke had inspired Williams with the courage of men like Helwys, pointed out the fallacy of the divine right of kings and explained the value and dignity of man which en-

4. Cathcart, 1250.

titled each to live in independence. But whether it was done in conversation with Coke or by some other circumstance, somehow the seeds of religious liberty were sown in the fertile mind of the youthful Roger Williams.

Williams went to Cambridge, mastered several languages, and was graduated in 1627. He was ordained in the Church of England, but it appears that he never actually served a parish. In disagreement with the state church, he took up Puritan beliefs and still later decided he was opposed to the principle of a state church and became a Separatist, leaving his homeland to seek freedom in America. Armitage quotes the old record:

> The ship Lyon, Mr. William Pierce master, arrived at Nantasket; she brought Mr. Williams, a godly minister, with his wife, Mr. Throgmorton, and others with their wives and children, about twenty passengers, and about two hundred tons of goods.[5]

Roger Williams, champion of religious liberty, arrived in the New World in 1631.

As the minister of teaching in the Boston Church, Williams outspokenly proclaimed his views on liberty, in full knowledge of earlier rules about banishment for such actions. Banishment not only meant that one must leave the territory around Boston, but to return would mean certain execution. Williams went to Salem after a delay until his child was born. They named her Freeborn Williams.

Friendly with the Indians and the Pilgrims, Williams spent a whole winter avoiding the Massachusetts order to arrest him and return him to England in chains. By spring, four other men of his conviction had joined him, and together they came to some freshwater springs in Narragansett Indian country. Williams named the place Providence in thanksgiving to God that He had brought them to this place of freedom. He bought land from the Indians and, with twelve men and their families, built a colony dedicated to liberty. Later this territory would be called Rhode Island.

Williams and his friends studied the Scriptures and, since

5. Thomas Armitage, A History of the Baptists (New York: Bryan, Taylor and Company, 1890), 626.

all had been part of the Church of England, came to a new conclusion that their infant baptism (sprinkling) had not been true,
Biblical baptism. There was not a church in the entire New
World that practiced adult believer's immersion. How could it
be accomplished? Williams was a minister, and there were no
others among them. They decided that there was only one
course of action available to them. Ezekiel Holliman immersed
Williams and Williams immersed Holliman and ten others. The
date of March 1639 marks the formation of this, the first Baptist church in America.

In 1637, a man came to America who would leave a more
enduring mark upon the Baptist movement in America. Dr.
John Clarke, a young medical doctor in London, believed
Christ was supreme and that English law kept him from freely
acknowledging his belief. He thought that he would find
freedom to express his views in America—religious liberty
would be his! Arriving in Boston in November, he was shocked
to find a new kind of religious intolerance. He met Anne Hutch-
inson, a religious teacher's daughter, who had come in conflict
with the Puritans over doctrine and had been denounced as
dangerous and a servant of Satan. She and her brother were
banished. While Clarke did not agree with her position on doctrine, he did believe deeply in her right to hold her beliefs. He
and a few others went voluntarily into banishment with the
Hutchinsons. After some years of wilderness wandering, they
came to Providence, purchased land from the Indians and
drew up a contract dedicating their lives, their holdings and
their land to Jesus Christ. In addition, they made freedom the
rule in their new home, which they called Newport.

Just when Clarke became a Baptist is not clear, but it is
reasonable to assume that Roger Williams's teaching influenced him as he gradually adopted Baptist views. At any rate,
Clarke and his followers formed the second Baptist church in
America in Newport, Rhode Island. The remaining church
records go back as far as 1648.

The early growth of the Baptists, while small by modern
standards, was rapid enough to be threatening to the Massachusetts Colony. In 1644, the leaders of the Massachusetts Colony wrote a stern law using "Anabaptist" (re-baptizers) as a

derogatory term for these nonconforming people. They were called "troublers of the church," teachers of "errors and heresies," and the law called for banishment of any who opposed baptism of infants or would go about seducing others from having their infants baptized. Childers says that:

> When the writers of the 1644 law in the Massachusetts Colony used the term Anabaptist they were doing it partly to decry the Baptists, partly to kindle and continue prejudice, and partly to bolster themselves and their position by the old and feeble device of belittling others.[6]

The law was rigorously enforced, and one of the most celebrated cases involved Clarke, Obadiah Holmes and John Crandall. The three had traveled from Newport to Lynn, Massachusetts, because they had been invited by some men there who had accepted Baptist views. The very small group worshiped on a Sunday in a private home. The meeting was interrupted by constables with warrants for the arrest of "certain . . . strangers."

Clarke, Holmes and Crandall were taken to the Established Church where they were tried and sentenced. Clarke was given a choice of a fine of twenty pounds or a whipping. Someone paid his fine. Crandall, a fine of five pounds or a whipping. Someone paid his fine. Interestingly, the two men who had sympathized with them were also arrested and fined. Holmes was offered a fine of thirty pounds (because he had been arrested before) or a whipping. Holmes refused an offer to pay his fine and was severely beaten by whipping. *The Baptist Encyclopedia* quotes from the record of Governor Joseph Jenks:

> Mr. Holmes was whipped with thirty stripes, and in such an unmerciful manner that in many days, if not some weeks, he could take no rest, but as he lay upon his knees and elbows, not being able to suffer any part of his body to touch the bed whereon he lay.[7]

After returning to Newport, Clarke and his friends were

6. Childers, 23.
7. Cathcart, 539.

able to continue their worship in freedom. Clarke left the pastorate at Newport to help Roger Williams develop and secure a new charter for Rhode Island. Obadiah Holmes was ordained and assumed the duties as Clarke's successor at Newport. The new charter of Rhode Island was probably written by Clarke and secured somehow from the despotic King Charles II of England. Williams had gone with Clarke to England but returned to Providence, leaving the rest of the charter work to Clarke. The new charter was unique, for it provided for both civil and religious liberty as no other charter had ever done. In 1663, Clarke returned to Rhode Island with charter in hand, officially signed and sealed by the King of England. It read in part:

> That no person within the said colony, at anytime hereafter, shall be anywise molested, punished, disquieted, or called in question for any difference in opinion in matters of religion which do not actually disturb the civil peace of said colony; but that all and every person and persons may from time to time, and at all times hereafter, freely and fully have and enjoy his and their own judgements and consciences in matters of religious commitment. . . .[8]

Up until 1664, no Baptist churches had actually been established outside Rhode Island. Persecutions had kept people with Baptist beliefs from openly organizing into churches. In 1664 a Welsh minister led a group of his fellow countrymen to Rehoboth, Massachusetts. John Miles (or Myles) and others had been forced to leave Wales because the Act of Uniformity (1662) compelled them to give up their relationship to their church and no longer carry out their personal convictions. Miles could have sacrificed his convictions and associated with the national church, but he chose to maintain his position and came to America for freedom to worship according to the dictates of his conscience. His group brought their church records with them, making them an official church from the beginning. The American Swanzey Baptist Church thus was a transplant from Swanzey, Wales. Miles was courageous in the face of op-

8. Ibid., 229.

position and gave fine counsel to the Boston believers who were suffering greatly for their views. Nearly one hundred years after his death one wrote of him, "his memory is still precious among us."[9]

Sixteen sixty-five saw a group of Baptist believers meeting in the home of Thomas Gould in Boston. Each of these seven men and two women had had some experience of fine, imprisonment or some other form of persecution. Gould is said to have been imprisoned so often and for such long periods that his health was impaired. In the face of all this, the little group erected a church building where they worshiped even though at least one time the doors were nailed shut by the courts of the magistrates. By 1671 there were twenty-two members.

The growth of the church was aided by some difficulties from which the Baptists profited. Four Quakers had been hanged in Boston. The word received in England brought an arousal of justice among the British and Massachusetts was ordered to send all prisoners back to England. The order was followed, and the Boston prisons were emptied of religious prisoners. In 1691 the new charter for Massachusetts was given under the hand of the new English Crown of William and Mary. Plymouth and Massachusetts Bay were made into a single colony. The Baptists were given toleration but still would have to pay the church tax. The Baptist movement kept working to free itself from supporting an institutional church with which it disagreed, but at least they could now worship without harassment.

The first Baptist church in the South was begun in 1690 in Charlestown, South Carolina, and before 1700 there were Baptist churches in New Jersey, New York, Pennsylvania and what is now Delaware. By the opening of the war between England and the Colonies over American independence, there were at least 35,000 Baptists in the New World.

The Revolutionary War provided the Baptists with exceptional opportunities. Naturally they were in favor of independence from England because of religious oppression,

9. Ibid., 791.

and this position ultimately increased their acceptability among other colonists. The Baptist cause for religious liberty was enhanced because they could point out the contradiction in gaining civil liberty without liberty for religion. New York developed a new constitution in 1777 granting "the free exercise of religious profession and worship without discrimination or preference." Colony after colony followed this lead until the Constitution of the United States held a first amendment in 1789 providing that "Congress shall make no law respecting an establishment of religion, or prohibit the free exercise thereof." Assuredly, this amendment was not solely a Baptist victory, but it did reflect what the Baptists had been saying since 1609, "The king is mortall man . . . and hath no power over ye imortall souls of his subjects. . . ."

At the beginning of the nineteenth century, a wide stretch of land, inhabited only by Indians, was open for expansion all the way to the great Mississippi River. Challenged, many adventurous families loaded up their wagons and headed for the vast frontiers.

Soon, shiploads of newcomers, interested in settling the West, were the accepted pattern at eastern ports. And all through the frontiers the Baptists established churches. A minister would take up a piece of land, carve out his own homestead, settle down and become the undershepherd of a Baptist flock. The Methodists were out there, but they had itinerant preachers riding a circuit so that worship services were infrequent. The more stately Presbyterians found their work more suitable to city life and rarely ventured over the Appalachians. The Catholics were mainly along the river routes where they established schools and mission activity in connection with the French trading enterprises. Thus the Baptists could worship regularly and without interference.

In a later chapter, we will see that the word of William Carey's efforts in far-off India challenged Americans toward missionary work. Ann and Adoniram Judson, Harriett and Samuel Newell and Luther Rice became the first Americans to hear and heed God's call "to the ends of the earth."

Meanwhile, something was happening along the Eastern Seaboard. A Second Great Awakening had begun and was moving toward the frontier. There had been a First Great Awakening back in 1725 with great preachers like Jonathan Edwards and George Whitefield and a lesser-known Gilbert Tennent, but the Revolutionary War had interrupted the revival emphasis and zeal. After the war, a spiritual disillusionment caused a decline in religious interest. But there is something magical about a new century—old problems are forgotten and great visions of the future take up the minds of men and women, boys and girls.

The Second Great Awakening relied upon the average pastors in the East and South and out on the frontiers instead of eloquent preachers with capabilities in mass psychology. The latter were no less important, but their methodology was different—preaching deep conviction of sin, a great need for repentance and faith and salvation in order to escape great judgment at the hand of a wrathful God. The men of the Second Great Awakening were less assuming, less itinerant, less emotional and less polished. They were, however, no less zealous for the cause of Christ. They were frontier preachers, brought up among common people; they labored as others to care for their family needs and expected little or no remuneration or special recognition for their preaching. Their faith and example turned the farmers and other workmen to Jesus Christ, and these in turn were given the desire to share the gospel whether as preachers or missionaries or faithful workers in their various occupations.

One of the great missionary leaders on the frontier was John Mason Peck, who went to what is now St. Louis, Missouri. This was the edge of the civilized world in 1817. Under the auspices of the Baptist Foreign Mission Board, Peck began a school in the back of a store. There he also began to preach and pray—sometimes alone, other times with a very few, sometimes under ridicule, other times amid total disinterest. Two months after he began, he held the first baptism of a convert, the mighty Mississippi River serving as the baptismal waters.

As the years passed, Peck traveled all around the frontier preaching and teaching, starting Baptist churches, establishing a seminary in Rock Spring, Illinois (which would later be moved to a new location and called Shurtleff College), and editing the *Western Pioneer* weekly religious paper. So positive were Peck's talents and faithful his service that he was given an honorary doctorate by Harvard College and University in 1852.

Up until about 1840, the Baptist movement in America was highly evangelistic, strong in home and foreign mission development, preferring denominational work but willing to cooperate interdenominationally if needed, concerned for education and desiring to keep the West from Catholicism. Such was the Baptist growth by 1844 that Torbet reports a total membership of 720,046 in 9,385 churches, with 6,364 ministers.[10] That computes out to be an increase of 360 percent from 1814 to 1844, during which time the population growth of the United States was at 140 percent.

Baptists were not without serious struggle during the years between the Revolution and the war between the states. Numerous Baptist bodies began associations emphasizing some specific item of theology or practice. There were also conflicts over:

1. Methods of evangelism
2. The doctrine of Unitarianism
3. The doctrine of Universalism or Universal Restoration
4. The influence of anti-mission thinking
5. Alexander Campbell and baptismal regeneration
6. The influx of Reformed theology men into Baptist pulpits
7. Hyper-Calvinism
8. The Masonic Lodge
9. The Bible Society and translating *baptizo* as "immersion"
10. Millerism and its prediction of the soon-coming end of the world
11. Old Landmarkism teaching that only Baptists were Christians
12. The slavery problem and the Civil War

While most of the problems were not sweeping enough to create a thorough challenge to all Baptists, the slavery problem

10. Torbet, *History of Baptists*, 253.

created a large division. The two Great Awakenings had aroused a wide humanitarian interest and concern, and most denominational groups accepted Negroes into their membership without difficulty. At the end of the Revolutionary War some question had already been raised about whether slavery was a valid practice for Christians. The Ketockton Association in Virginia resolved in 1787 that "hereditary slavery was a breach of the divine law." Some asked legislatures to pass abolition measures of various degrees. The Northern Baptist churches and associational leadership were strongly sympathetic with abolitionism.

Southern Baptists, however, saw the problem in a very different light. They were bothered by what they felt was antislavery propaganda from the North. Before these pressures came, the Baptists generally had been willing to give up their slavery practices. But now, with increased Northern influence, the Southern Baptists through their associations pressured state legislatures against the abolition of slavery. This was a natural turn to defensiveness of their institution of slavery. Some became radical and began to threaten the lives of abolitionist "strangers" who had come into their communities. Other groups of clergymen were passing resolutions in defense of slave holding.

There were two climactic events that broke Baptists into Northern and Southern designations. The first involved a situation with Lane Theological Seminary and Oberlin College. A new antislavery emphasis was beginning in Ohio under the leadership of Theodore Weld. There are few and sketchy reports of this action, but Torbet gleaned the essentials. Mr. Weld, a convert to Christianity under the revival preaching of Charles Finney, was an abolitionist leader who began attending Lane Theological Seminary in Ohio. He, and others, "fraternized" with the Negroes around the community. The problem was compounded by a man who supported the seminary financially and also encouraged Weld in his abolitionist efforts. When the actions of Weld and his friends became the object of criticism, most of the abolitionist students moved to Oberlin College with the understanding that Finney would become professor of theology. This event served to make antislavery a part of the revivalist movement. Weld and his associates worked through the local churches to gain support and influenced sentiments from Ohio eastward after 1832.[11]

There followed a series of lesser significant events. In 1835 Robert Daniel expressed a need for a southern convention. In 1839 a Southern Baptist home mission society had been launched, but it failed with the death of its founder in 1842. Dr. W. C. Buck in Kentucky explored the possibility of a Western Baptist convention in 1840. These ideas indicate that there were already tendencies toward a division of Baptists along sectional lines. Meanwhile, American Baptist Antislavery Conventions were held in New York (1840) and Baltimore (1841).

The second climactic event actually caused the schism among American Baptists. The Triennial Convention of American Baptists met in Philadelphia in 1844. An abolitionist moderate, Dr. Francis Wayland, of Rhode Island, was elected president. Some members of the convention wanted to discuss the slavery question on the convention floor. A few Southern delegates, led chiefly by Dr. Richard Fuller, a slave-holding minister from South Carolina, recommended that the convention restrict itself to a discussion of foreign missions. The decision on this matter was predictable because, of the 460 delegates, only eight were from south of the Mason-Dixon line. A strange decision was made that foreign missions should be conducted impartially, but that individuals could feel free to express and promote whatever views each held. This action certainly was cause for Southern Baptist fears. Subsequently, the board of managers of the Triennial Convention gave a reply to the Alabama Convention that was a total departure from what they had said a few months earlier: "If anyone should offer himself as a missionary, having slaves, and should insist on retaining them as his property, we could not appoint him. One thing is certain, we can never be a party to any arrangement which would imply approbation of slavery."[12]

Debate began almost immediately on this statement, and the Baptist Home Mission Society decided in April 1845 that it

11. Ibid., 286-287.
12. Ibid., 291.

would be best for the work to be done by separate mission organizations—one in the North and one in the South. A convention was called for, to be held in May, and 328 delegates from Southern Baptist churches met in Augusta, Georgia, to organize the Southern Baptist Convention. The organization called for denominational boards of control over the affairs of the convention—a significant departure from the associational methods previously used. Missionary activity, for instance, was to be directed by the Southern Baptist Home and Foreign Mission *Board*, not through an independent Baptist mission *society*. Here was an example of a basic philosophical and ideological difference which would produce conflict between Northern associational Baptists and the Southern Baptist Convention.

The Civil War kept the sectional rivalry strong. The Northern Baptists supported the Union and the Southern Baptists, of course, did not. The Baptists of the North supported the war emotionally, and many of their young men served in the Union army. The Philadelphia Association wholeheartedly supported the Emancipation Proclamation and almost immediately set about raising money through the American Baptist Home Mission Society to aid the freed slaves of the South. One of their main methods of aid was supporting special schools to help Negroes become preachers and teachers among their own race. Programs of aid were extremely limited in both North and South during the very difficult years of reconstruction because of the devastated economy.

It is understandable that, in spite of the Northern Baptist overtures of assistance in the postwar years, the Southern Baptist Convention voted to remain a separate organization. However, the two groups did hope to have cordial and congenial relationships between them. Among the things that kept them apart were the constant sectionalism and the great difference in polity.

Baptist growth in America was great and advanced until the 1840s, when conflict damaged the spirit and the zeal. The war years and reconstruction drained most of the strength from religious expansion until the turn of the century. Turning inward temporarily, the Baptists began consolidating their beliefs and indoctrinating their youth, finally culminating in the formation of the Baptist Young People's Union (B.Y.P.U.) in 1891.

From that day in 1639 in Providence when Roger Williams, Ezekiel Holliman and ten others were baptized and the first Baptist church in America was begun, the numerical growth among Baptists has been strong. By 1900 there were approximately 33,000 Baptist churches in America with a combined membership of over three million. The twentieth century would bring new and different tensions with their accompanying adjustments.

8

Baptist Expansion on the European Continent

His lamp am I
  To shine where He shall say.
And lamps are not for sunny rooms,
  Nor for the light of day;
But for dark places of the earth,
Where shame and wrong and crime have birth;
Or for the murky twilight gray,
Where wandering sheep have gone astray;
Or where the light of faith grows dim
And souls are groping after Him;
And sometimes, a flame,
  Clear shining through the night,
So bright we do not see the lamp,
  But only see the light.
So may I shine—His light the flame—
That men may glorify His name.

—Anonymous

A review of the work of the Baptists on the European continent must begin with some insights into the unique character of the European nations. Somehow, in Western, American provincialism, it is difficult to understand that there are others in the world with a valid, although different,

perspective on things. To some degree, this lack of understanding has been a negative factor in missions, political, social
and economic intercourse. To understand the spread of Baptist beliefs and practices on the Continent means that their
basic ideals and heritage must be comprehended.

The general political philosophy in Europe has been one of
some form of autocratic rule over a number of obedient subjects. The idea of a crown, a strong central government and
sovereign control is highly respected. This heritage produces a
people who are followers. In some ways this concept gives a
clue as to why European countries were willing to accept
Charlemagne, Louis XIV, Napoleon Bonaparte, the Czars,
Elizabeth I, Hitler and Stalin. This political ideology has pre-
vailed for more than one thousand years, in direct opposition
to the Baptist belief in the complete separation of church and
state. So intertwined were church and state in Europe that Charlemagne was more informed in theology than most religious
leaders of the early ninth century. During the medieval period,
many of these great leaders, such as St. Olaf of Norway and St.
Stephan of Hungary, were canonized by the Roman church.

Also, for over one thousand years Christianity (that is, the
Roman church) closely paralleled the political order in organization. The Roman church has used the Roman Empire's government as a model for its ecclesiastical hierarchy from the beginning.

Not only the Roman church was administratively and bu-
reaucratically dominant, but the Reformation also established
itself under the leadership of strong and capable men. Calvin
was strong as a preacher-teacher, writer and military leader, as
the Huguenot movement testifies. Zwingli, too, was a great
preacher-teacher with military expertise in Switzerland and
Bavaria. Luther was a strong preacher-teacher and musician
and had great ability in exerting the power of the pen, because
his political world was significantly decentralized at that time. It
is understandable that when Baptists introduced their concept
of the soul-liberty of the believer and the sovereignty of the
local church, they did not find a very ready acceptance.

The Eastern Orthodox church never really had a Reformation at all, so Greece and the Slavic world have to this date a

strong ecclesiastical organization. A few years ago, when this writer visited a pastor-friend in Athens, he discovered that the Orthodox church there controls all aspects of religious life. The evangelicals cannot propagate their faith by use of tracts, newspaper articles or invitations, radio or television programs, or even phone calls. The pastor-friend's comments made a vivid impression: "Everything we do must be done within the walls of our church. We cannot use the open methods you use in America, because we do not know who is an 'informer.'" A professor at a university in Athens confessed that he could not even be sure that his wife or children were not "informers." If this is true in a relatively free nation like Greece, it is not at all difficult to comprehend the lack of religious freedom in the Communist-dominated countries. Deeply ingrained ways of life prohibit the spread of the Baptist faith and practice in other cultures.

There are other factors, especially in some parts of southern and eastern Europe, that have hampered the Baptist cause. Although now greatly improved, widespread illiteracy made the Baptist principle of "freedom to participate" difficult to put into operation, because it required an ability to read the Scriptures. Illiteracy has long been a great foe of freedom, the democractic process and most reforms.

Legalism (another powerful foe of freedom) of both church and state served to maintain conformity among the common people. The Roman church, for example, published the *Index* of forbidden books and material, and national political sovereigns ruled with tyranny under the guise of the divine right of kings.

Somehow it is not surprising that some subjects would refuse to continue submitting to the oppressive orders of the religious and political institutions. An age-old principle declares, Oppression always breeds revolution. And Europeans burst into attempts of freedom during the Renaissance and the Reformation, only to find the strong cultural influences leading them back to a dominance of little different nature.

Even in the decades since the second world war, with the strong international desire for all sorts of freedom, the Baptist movement has not been highly accepted. Religions of many varieties are confusing, and many of the traditional churches are not meeting individual needs, so all movements are suspect. Of course, the lack of Biblical morality would naturally be opposed to the Baptist teaching of the subjection of the believer-priest to the Lordship of Jesus Christ.

It is amazing that the Baptist testimony managed to gain a foothold at all in Europe, but it did. Christian "salt" and Biblical truth combined to bring the Baptist movement to much of the European world. In God's time, He always prepares situations and matches them with qualified men to accomplish His work. The beginning and expansion of the Baptist system on the European continent was no exception.

Into this vast entrenched culture came a man named Johann Gerhard Oncken. Rushbrooke indicates that the British refer to Oncken as the "Father of German Baptists," but that a far more accurate name would be the "Father of the Continental Baptists."[1] Oncken had a checkered background, filled with struggles and numerous griefs. After his conversion he desired to serve his Savior but again met with adversity and pain. He was still able, however, to keep his goals clearly before him and developed a durable Baptist testimony over many areas of Europe.

Oncken was born in northwest Germany in 1800. His father had been forced to leave Germany just prior to Johann's birth because he had participated in political activities advocating the overthrow of Napoleon. When young Oncken reached his fourteenth year, he was confirmed in the Lutheran church and there learned the habit of attending church regularly. Soon after Napoleon's power over Germany had been broken, a Scottish merchant came to Oncken's hometown to collect payment for materials that had previously been smuggled into Germany. Somehow he liked this German boy and asked him to come to Scotland where he might "make a man of him."[2] For the next nine years Oncken worked with his Scottish benefactor, traveling over the British Isles, France and Ger-

---

1. J. H. Rushbrooke, *The Baptist Movement in the Continent of Europe* (London: the Kingsgate Press, 1923), 17.
2. Ibid., 19.

many. One of the first things this man did for Oncken was to give him a Bible.

In Britain, with his Bible, Oncken was influenced by the Presbyterians, from whom he learned to appreciate worship. He later went to live with an Independent family near London, whose family prayers, church worship and fellowship impressed him. It was during this time that he became a Christian, upon the occasion of visiting a Methodist service where a sermon on Romans 8:1 was given. His conversion was thorough, and he gave his life to the Lordship of Christ for the purpose of spreading the gospel.

He was a very conscientious and devoted believer, with the zeal that is often true of new Christians. In his case, however, the zeal did not lessen as his years passed. He purchased tracts with most of his lunch money and distributed them widely. In 1823, under the Continental Society, he returned to Germany as a missionary and settled in Hamburg as a member of the English Reformed Church. The pastor, Mr. Matthews, encouraged him and gave him opportunities to speak.

Oncken's first real sermon was given before eighteen people, but it resulted in the conversion of a man about his own age who would become his lifelong friend and aid—C. F. Lange. This kind of preaching in private homes was not acceptable to the German authorities, especially when within two months the house was overcrowded and popular interest kept increasing. The police said that they could no longer meet in private homes, so Oncken began preaching on street corners, in restaurants and anywhere else he could get a few listeners. The local clergy as well as the police were annoyed, and Oncken believed they would put him out of the city. To counter such action, he opened a bookstore and became registered as a citizen of Hamburg.

For ten years his Lutheran, Presbyterian, Independent, Methodist and English Reformed background encouraged him in his work with the Edinburgh Bible Society and the Evangelical Alliance. With boundless energy he distributed Bibles, preached when he could, assisted the pastor at St. George (the church he attended) and with aid from the British Sunday School Union began the first Sunday School in Germany.

Up until this point, Oncken had had no known contact with Baptists. In 1826 he went to Bremen, where a number of pastors who supported him in his evangelistic work encouraged him to take some theological training toward becoming a clergyman—they would pay his expenses. Oncken declined their offer because he already had some doubts about infant baptism, which they practiced. His doubts grew as he studied his Bible on his own, and when his first child was born he did not have it baptized. He began corresponding with different men regarding how he could become immersed. One told him to baptize himself, another said he could come to England to be baptized, and so on—none of which seemed to him satisfactory. In the providence of God, Oncken made friends with Calvin Tubbs, the captain of an American cargo vessel. When Tubbs returned to America and told his story to the American Baptist Foreign Mission Society in Boston, its representative repeated the story to Professor Barnas Sears at what is now Madison University. The Baptist Encyclopedia reports that in 1833 Sears went to Germany to further his studies, and, "while there he baptized the Rev. Mr. Oncken, whose zealous and self-denying labors have been so abundantly blessed in the spread of pure Christianity, and in the gathering together of so large a Baptist membership."[3] Rushbrooke confirms that in April of 1834, Oncken, his wife and five others were immersed in the Elbe River in Hamburg.[4]

Persecution had been great before, but it had come mostly from civil authorities. After Oncken's immersion, and the formation of the first Baptist church in Germany at Hamburg, persecution began from the very people among whom Oncken's ministry had been so great. The Evangelical Society with which he had worked disowned him, the school he had begun put him out and his connection with the Independent church was broken. Then came a climactic event. In 1837, Oncken performed his first baptismal service in broad daylight (heretofore they had been semiprivate evening events) in the Elbe River, at which a riot broke out, and the Baptists were then officially for-

3. Cathcart, Baptist Encyclopedia, 1038.
4. Rushbrooke, 22.

bidden to worship in public. Private assembly was tolerated, but tickets of admission were required. In these difficult times, the Baptist numbers grew to nearly one hundred by the end of 1838.

The next year, and on several occasions in years to come, Oncken and his friends Julius Kobner and C. F. Lange were imprisoned, forced to pay the court costs and had goods seized and sold. The local Senate even volunteered to pay the costs if Oncken would go to America. Sentiment from England and the United States poured in and, fearing economic conflict, the Hamburg Senate again allowed private worship.

The work grew rapidly, and Oncken ventured to rent a large granary which was converted into a bookstore, Sunday School and chapel. The people prayed that the opening would be delivered from persecution, but the answer came unexpectedly. On May 5, 1842, history records a great fire in Hamburg in which one-third of the city burned, leaving many, many people homeless. Oncken offered his granary to the authorities as a refuge center for the victims. The Baptist "sectarians" proved themselves brave and self-sacrificing as they cared for about seventy refugees for several months. The city officials gave a letter of thanks to Oncken and, except for a few instances of minor conflict with other clergymen, the Baptists had at last won their freedom to worship according to the dictates of their conscience.

During the years of persecution and afterward, Oncken traveled widely, and his name became associated with the formation of Baptist churches all over Germany, East Prussia, Denmark, Sweden, Holland, Switzerland, Russia, the Balkans and Hungary while he was a representative of the American Baptist Foreign Mission Society. He also made many trips to England and one to America, seeking funds for European Baptist work. At last, this energetic evangelist, organizer, book publisher and salesman, pioneer in German ministerial training and servant of the Savior, died in Zurich on January 2, 1884.

When considering the indigenous nature of Baptist churches, certain local qualities appear. Oncken generated in the German Baptists a deep religious earnestness, a sense of the grace of God in their lives, a fervent love for the Scriptures, a passion for souls, considerable detail in organization, a native abundant physical energy, persuasiveness in speech and a warmly gracious reaching out to open the hearts of men.

German Baptists treasure the memory of their *keblatt* (clover-leaf), a triumvirate of leadership consisting of Oncken the organizer, Kobner the musical theologian and G. W. Lehmann the diplomat. These three worked harmoniously together in the spread of Baptist Christianity in and around Germany. It would be difficult to contain within these pages any further biographical material of the "clover-leaf," but each in his way contributed to the furtherance of God's gospel in Europe.

GERMANY

From Hamburg, the Baptists spread out over Germany as people came to the city to hear the gospel, were saved, given literature and returned home to witness of the gospel truth and establish Baptist churches. Before 1848, this scene had repeated itself at least twenty-six times, resulting in a total membership of fifteen hundred. Such was the growth under persecution from the state church and the state police.

In 1848 and again in 1850, German constitutional documents were published granting individual freedom of religious belief, freedom of religious fellowship in communities and freedom of family and public worship. The measures also provided for independence of civil functions and matters of faith —a kind of separation of church and state. In a single moment of time, the local churches were able to come out of their hiding places into evangelical freedom. Flags began appearing on houses in a wave of patriotic demonstration, and from the highest towers Christian choral music to the glory of God filled the cities.

As a result, missionary activity moved out in all directions, and the local churches established greater organizational structures. Oncken offered a wise comment regarding their new opportunities:

> If hitherto we have needed grace to suffer and to endure, we need it doubly now for joyous and full self-

dedication to the work of spreading the gospel.[5]
A valuable word of advice for then and today, for there is always the tendency to relax into complacency during times of ease.

The Baptists heeded well, and with enthusiasm expanded their efforts. A missionary magazine was begun and distributed, the Sunday School organization was becoming contagious and local churches were organizing into associations. Wilhelm Weist was the first national missionary of the Union of Associated Churches of Baptized Christians in Germany and Denmark (1848). The union was developed under G. W. Lehmann's careful guidance, respecting local church sovereignty but uniting the churches in evangelistic endeavor.

As the 1850s dawned, a threatening political struggle took place. King Frederick William IV was swaying under pressures both for and against religious tolerance. Deputations came from France, America, England and the evangelicals and Baptists on the Continent, urging in favor of religious liberty for all. The Evangelical and Protestant Alliances proposed forming a combined convention and met in Paris (1855), with Lehmann and Kobner attending. From this convention a deputation met with the king in Cologne, and he promised a full and immediate investigation of the facts in all the German states. Another Alliance convention met in Berlin in 1857, which the king was invited to attend. Plans were made and about to be carried out to this end, but the king's failing health afforded only a farewell audience for a single representative of the Alliance. Within a few days, Prince Wilhelm assumed the royal duties as regent, and a new era was born. New policies were put into operation:

1. Attacks on religious assemblies were forbidden.

2. Children of Baptists were no longer forced to receive religious instruction in school.

3. Local churches were permitted to incorporate (1875).

During the 1860s, general persecution died out except for a few localized situations.

Four great cities produced most of the Baptist leadership (Hamburg, Berlin, Konigsberg and Bremen), and the prosperity

5. *Ibid.*, 35.

of advancement continued to the turn of the century. About that time, the state church resurged in the form of many imitations of "dissenter" practices, such as the Sunday School, youth work and prayer meetings. These imitations tended to cause those state church people who had been converted under Baptist teaching to remain in their churches and not separate from them.

Oncken had realized the need for the preparation of Christian ministers. However, the idea was slow to take root because of a genuine fear of ecclesiasticism, which might detract from the priesthood of the individual believer and the free operation of the Holy Spirit. For nearly thirty years Oncken invited young potential ministers to take a six-month course under his direction in Hamburg. By 1880, an expanded curriculum was in place, and a four-year seminary had become an actuality.

The first world war brought extremes to Germany. German rationalism had already produced indifference to faith, the true gospel and evangelistic appeal among the professional clergy. Instead, there came an intellectualism that addressed the lives of a particular elite, and the churches were left without a relevant message. Human reason based upon philosophical interpretations of Scripture replaced the urgency of the gospel. Man could do it without God! This idea was set aside for a while, because the arrival of a tragic war and national peril reawakened the need for God. Churches were filled during this time, but by the end of the war the old indifference had returned. In the struggle of reconstruction following the war, the indifference turned into a hatred for God. A lost war, an economic disaster—why had God done this? The churches were nearly empty, preaching seemed powerless, and very few were being saved. During the war many, if not most, of the pastors served in the army, and without their leadership the churches faltered. Children grew up without parental direction, education or discipline because of the demands of the war effort.

Another earmark of the 1918-1920 era in Germany was the turning away from and scoffing at of morals supported by religious teaching. The people gave themselves freely to nearly a full year (1920) of the pursuit of sheer human pleasure. Nineteen twenty-one saw the people turn briefly from sin and evil, and large numbers listened carefully to the gospel and were converted. But the harsh realities of economic woe and the awful Treaty of Versailles brought about either new hatreds or renewed hatreds, or both.

To these dark moments, one desperate note must be added for the Baptists—the loss by death of four very key leaders in twelve months beginning in September 1921: Hermann Renner, a leading Baptist philanthropist from Hamburg; Carl Mascher, the director of German foreign mission efforts for twenty years; J. G. Lehmann, the son of Oncken's friend, who gave many years to literary work and evangelism especially among the Russian prisoners of war (over two thousand were converted and baptized in prison camps); and Gustav Gieselbusch, the gifted and influential head of the seminary in Hamburg. Such losses created a vacuum in leadership.

The Baptists were not greatly concerned about the rise of Nazism in the 1920s and 1930s because of their dedication to the separation of church and state. Neither did the movement curb their evangelistic efforts until after 1934. When the Baptist World Alliance met in Georgia (U.S.A.) in 1939, German Baptists were warned not to attend. Actually, the German Baptists had withdrawn from facing the deep spiritual needs of the day and the potential consequences of totalitarianism.

The second world war brought destruction of half of the Baptist church buildings in the west of Germany and almost total destruction in the east. The seminary at Hamburg was reduced to rubble and the publications offices and plant at Kassel were demolished. But the Baptist congregations courageously emerged from the war with a desire to share in spiritual reconstruction, and they were aided by the fact that very few of them had cooperated with Hitler's National Socialist Party. Churches were rebuilt in the west, new congregations were started and the literature division was restored in 1950. In that year there were 100,219 members of German Baptist congregations.

DENMARK

Julius Kobner, one of the Oncken *keblatt*, is most responsible for the rise of Baptist work in Denmark. Some earlier churchmen had come to this small nation planting seeds of the gospel, as well as doubts about the rationalism so prevalent among the clergy. Kobner learned of a man in Copenhagen named Monster, who had been converted through some traveling mission groups and through studying the Scriptures on his own. Monster had come to reject infant baptism even though he had never met any Baptists. Kobner immersed Monster and ten others and the first Baptist church in Denmark began in 1839.

Severe persecution followed because the government strictly forbade such meetings. A year later, when Oncken and Kobner returned to Copenhagen, they saw ten more persons brought into the tiny church. The two met with a small group of believers in Langeland where hatred was very strong against the Baptists. The civil leaders put out a warrant and offered a reward for the arrest of the two visitors, but they escaped without being taken.

New groups of Baptists sprang up as relatives witnessed to family members in other parts of the land, but the government countered with great persecution by imprisoning pastors and other lay-leaders. Oncken presented the king of Denmark a petition on behalf of the Baptists in 1841, but it was several months before they were set free, and then with a stern prohibition against their continued preaching. Many preachers ignored the ban on their preaching and were imprisoned again. Not until 1849, when a new and liberal constitution was adopted containing liberty of conscience provisions, was persecution to become unlawful.

The entrance of Mormonism, especially in the cities, caused some trouble for the Baptists, but there was a general Baptist expansion until about 1900. The decline which followed closely paralleled that of their German neighbors. Today there are a little more than four thousand Baptists in Denmark, with a seminary and college located near Copenhagen. It appears that the Baptists in Denmark did not have great evangelistic success, but where they did grow and construct churches, the edifices were very beautiful and enduring.

SWEDEN

Evangelical work laid a preparatory groundwork for the beginning of Baptist churches in Sweden. Near the end of the sixteenth century, Lutheranism became the official state religion, and strict laws were enforced to make the inhabitants conform. At first this was purely a matter of a state church repressing anyone who professed a strong religious life of faith and piety. During the seventeenth century, however, Baptists were influenced by the Pietist movement, which brought an emphasis on Christian living but did so within the Lutheran state church. There was some persecution of those who spoke against sin and worldiness, but since this was not illegal they could not be imprisoned. One method used to strike against this kind of unauthorized preaching was to declare the preacher insane and commit him to an asylum.

In the early eighteenth century, some parents were withholding their children from Lutheran infant baptism. On some occasions the babies were forcibly taken from the parents and sprinkled. Others of low influential status were imprisoned, some for more than twenty years. There is no evidence, however, that believer's baptism was practiced anywhere in Sweden at this time.

A Methodist missionary from England did work in Stockholm for twelve years. However, he was forced to leave after hostility resulted in a riotous assault upon him during one of his Sunday services. There were increasing numbers of true believers in some areas of Sweden who had apparently come to that knowledge by their independent study of Scripture while they were in the Lutheran church. Penalties were given for violating traditional church practices regarding the Lord's Supper and absolution, so some began celebrating the sacrament (ordinance) privately, which was severely punishable. The meetings in homes also included singing, reading one of Luther's sermons and prayers. A royal edict of 1726 invoked imprisonment and/or banishment for such offenders, and this condition remained until 1854.

The beginning of Baptist work in Sweden came near the end of this period of strict control. A Swedish sailor, G. W. Schroeder, was saved in a meeting in New Orleans and later became a member of the Baptist Mariner's Church in New York. American Baptists authorized Schroeder to be a missionary among the Swedish sailors. In this capacity he met F. O. Nilson, who apparently was already a believer but did not know about baptism. Schroeder encouraged him to study his New Testament on the matter, and in 1847 Nilson went to Hamburg to be immersed by Oncken. Returning to Sweden, Nilson persuaded some of his friends about believer's baptism. As a result, in 1848, with the aid of a Danish pastor, Nilson and five others began the first Baptist church in Sweden, in Gothenburg. Nilson was ordained in Hamburg and returned to pastor the growing flock. By the time they had fifty or so new members, Nilson was arrested, tried and condemned for preaching and leading others away from Lutheranism. In spite of humble appeals, Nilson was forced to leave Sweden, going to Denmark where he pastored the Baptist church in Copenhagen from 1851-1853. After a time in America with Swedish Baptists, the banishment was annulled and Nilson returned to Gothenburg, reorganized a Baptist church and became its pastor.

God had another man to take up the Baptist work after Nilson. Andreas Wiberg was converted under the Methodists while a student at the University of Uppsala. As a state church minister, he was warned, suspended and accused of heresy for accepting pietistic views. He joined the Pietists but was very alarmed at the influence of the Baptists in Sweden. In the process of writing a book against believer's baptism, his research led him to a defense of the Baptist view instead.

In 1855, a few men joined Wiberg, supported by the American Baptist Publication Society, to embark on a wider evangelistic work. Others joined with them, placing their emphasis on organizing Sunday Schools. Eighteen fifty-seven found arrangements being made for a Baptist conference, even though it was not in conformity with existing state laws. The nineteen people gathered without interference. The conference in 1858 involved about one hundred delegates. In 1861 a third conference was held, at which time it was reported that there were 125 Baptist churches in Sweden with a total of 4,930 members.[6]

In 1866, the Bethel Seminary in Sweden was begun under the auspices of the American Baptist Mission Society. The school and its graduates provided good leadership for Baptist expansion in Sweden.

Legislation today provides for religious liberty and recognition of the right to exist as lawful, independent churches. Even though the Lutheran church has great power and prestige as the state religion, with birth registration depending on state church baptism, Baptists are free to carry on their work today without direct legal, political interference, and the number of Baptists is increasing slowly.

FINLAND

The beginning of the Baptist movement in Finland differs from that in Denmark and Sweden in that there was no German Baptist influence. The comparatively few Baptists in Finland are divided into two distinct groups—a Swedish language group and a small and weak Finnish group.

The first Baptist church in Finland was a Swedish group begun in Jacobstad in 1869 upon the testimony of some Aland Island people. They were immersed believers who shared their faith before the archbishop at Abo. Their testimony was so interesting that one of the clergymen took them to his home for further discussion, which resulted in the conversion of his son and daughter. The new believers went to Stockholm for baptism, and this small group formed the new church.

The work among the Finns themselves began with the conversion of a sailor by the name of Henriksson somewhere in his foreign travels. He died two years after his return to Finland, and Esaias Lundburg (whom Henriksson had baptized) took the leadership of forming the Baptist church in Loria in 1870.

Although free from persecution, the Baptist movement had

6. Ibid., 93.

very slow growth, probably never reaching more than three thousand total members. Today, under the supervision of the Soviets, the work of the Baptists is very difficult to learn about.

NORWAY

In 1857, Fredrik Rymker, a Danish sailor, became the first Baptist missionary in Norway. He had become a Christian and was baptized while in America. In Norway, he settled near Skien, where some groundwork had already been laid by Rev. G. A. Lammers, the pastor of the Lutheran church there.

Lammers had been preaching with great power and eloquence the necessity of a personal acceptance of the Savior as the sole means of conversion. This was contrary to the Lutheran teaching of baptismal regeneration. His converts looked up to him with honor and respect, but the Lutheran denomination opposed his teaching. In 1856, Lammers and twenty-seven others organized what they called the Apostolic Free Church, and rapid growth soon brought the membership to one hundred. A dispute broke out among the Apostolic Free Church people over baptism of infants. Lammers was not in favor of rebaptism of those sprinkled in infancy, but nineteen others believed that the only valid baptism was believer's immersion. In September 1858, the nineteen were immersed in a lake near Skien—one man immersed another man, who in turn immersed all the others. These nineteen were excluded from the Free Church and formed what was essentially a Baptist church without any outside influence except their study of the New Testament. They called their group the Church of Christian Dissenters. Although they never identified themselves as Baptists, they had prepared the way for the advancement of Baptists into Norway.

In December 1858, Fredrik Rymker immersed a man named Carl Kongerod as his first convert, and by 1860 seven members had established the first Baptist church in Norway. Several small churches were begun, but many of them failed because of persecution and lack of leadership. Three years later, Rymker returned to Denmark, leaving the Baptists without leadership, even though they were very consecrated and dedicated believers.

Another Norwegian, Godtfred Hubert, had been saved and baptized in America, served in the American navy during the Civil War and returned to his native land in 1862. For about twenty years he preached in Norway with the support of the English Baptists. He founded, and began a missionary outreach from, a Baptist church in Bergen. In 1872, a district association was formed north of the Arctic Circle, and in 1877 the Norwegian Baptist Conference was begun with fourteen churches. By the turn of the century there were forty-two churches scattered over the country. In 1910, the Baptist Theological Seminary was started in Christiania, providing national preparation for its pastors and other leaders as well as for missionaries to foreign lands, especially in the Congo region of Africa.

The effects of two world wars hampered the Baptist expansion in Norway because economic problems limited church funding. It was not until 1930 that the Norwegian Baptists were able to support themselves without aid from other countries. The German occupation brought the need for relief for refugees, and the evangelistic emphasis declined. As a result, there has been a total of only sixty-three Baptist churches in Norway, and since then numerical losses have exceeded the gains.

POLAND, CZECHOSLOVAKIA, LATVIA
ESTONIA AND LITHUANIA

There is great difficulty in tracing the history of the Baptist movement in the central and eastern European world. Poland was opened to Baptist work by German missionary activity, but migration due to wars and invasions kept the groups from achieving much stability. The earliest date of any activity is 1858, when nine persons were saved and immersed at Adamow. State and religious officials persecuted these believers and thousands more later. However, their arrests and trials became opportunities to preach to judges, and imprisonment made possible a gospel witness to convicts. The greatest weakness of the Baptists in Poland was that the ministry was mostly among the German minority. There was very little impact among the Polish people themselves. American missionary funds helped keep the work going with aid to publications, orphanages and hospital outreach. Sadly, World War II practically destroyed the Baptist work in Poland and, under Communist domination, it has not been able to advance significantly.

Czechoslovakia—the land of the Bohemians and the martyr, John Hus—has a history of a love of religious freedom. The Moravian Brethren and the Anabaptist Hubmaier were active there prior to the Counter Reformation. A fierce armed battle ended in victory for the Catholics, who did not permit any sectarian groups to exist. The Lutherans were finally allowed to hold meetings in 1871, but repression continued strong. When a Baptist missionary from Britain, A. Meereis, held a Sunday School in Broumov, the police came in, expelled all worshipers, locked the building and jailed the preacher. Later, in 1877, Meereis baptized five believers at Brandys, but he was not allowed to continue the work. After World War I nearly all the leadership was gone because of the large number of war casualties. Assisted by Baptist missions from England and America, the work was revived somewhat but was never able to become completely self-supporting, even in times of liberty. World War II destroyed much of the remaining work and, because Czechoslovakia is a Communist satellite, the pressures make the Baptist efforts minimal.

Latvia, Estonia and Lithuania have a common history of persecution, suffering and yet promise for gospel promotion by the Baptists. Protestantism had been in Latvia around 1550, but the Baptists did not appear until after 1850. Small groups met for prayer and Bible reading, the participants being mostly women during the early part of the movement. During the Crimean War, a man named Jakobsohn went to Germany for employment, contacted the Baptists and was immersed there in 1855. He became the first Latvian Baptist, and from his influence and German Baptist aid, the spread of the gospel advanced. The first baptisms in Latvia were administered in 1861. The Russian domination since World War I has forbidden Baptists to meet. Lithuania has never had any significant Baptist movement, but Estonia seemed to be more fertile soil for the gospel until Russian domination, after which many believers were sent to Siberia for holding prayer meetings. Continued persecution by the government and the Roman Catholics, combined with economic woes, has severely hampered the Baptist movement in Estonia.

THE BALKAN AREA

There have never been more than a few Baptists in most of the Balkan area. Bulgaria has never had a national Baptist movement except among Russian immigrants. Rumanian Baptists have had periods of persecution from the state and hostile priests, but nearly full freedom was given to Baptists there in 1928. The Baptist World Alliance aided in establishing a Rumanian Baptist Convention, but it consisted partly of Rumanian, Hungarian, German and Russian elements. Baptists exist there today under strict government control.

Hungary enjoyed the largest advances of Baptists in southeastern Europe. Some artisans from Budapest had gone to Hamburg, Germany, for employment in 1845. There they were converted and baptized under Oncken's ministry. When they returned to Hungary in 1849, they told of their new-found faith. Heinrich Meyer, a German living in Budapest and an employee of the British and Foreign Bible Society (1873-1883), saw many conversions and baptisms, Sunday Schools established and the stage set for Baptist advancement. The next ten years saw nearly four thousand new converts and baptisms in Hungary, with the resulting establishment of local Baptist churches. Meyer unfortunately acted as a dictator, without preparing the churches for local autonomy. This, plus the economic and political fragmentation of Hungary by war and treaty, has caused the number of Baptists to fluctuate greatly.

Yugoslavia became an independent state after World War I, and the Southern Baptists from America served strongly there. Baptists from Germany caused some tension, and what Baptists there were mostly scattered in search of employment, leaving few churches. Divisions following World War II, plus

Communist dominance, have nearly ended Baptist work in Yugoslavia.

Greece has no Baptist work at all. The Greek Orthodox church and the state cooperate together to keep all other religions under complete control. Informer systems are maintained to prohibit expansion of any groups not approved.

SPAIN

Baptist work in this Roman Catholic-dominated country has been extremely limited. Baptist missionaries from America and Sweden have had minimal success. The Spanish Civil War (1936-1939) saw most churches and church equipment destroyed and about one-fourth of the members of Baptist churches killed. The political leadership of Spain places heavy restrictions on preaching, public services and visitation, in an effort to discourage anything other than Roman Catholic religious enterprises.

ITALY

About 1863, the Southern Baptist Foreign Mission Board and the London Baptist Missionary Society sought to establish Baptist mission work in Italy. By 1905, there were only about fourteen hundred converts, and in 1923 the London Baptists left the country. The Southern Baptists by 1939 were only contributing funds for Italians working among their own people. Persecution by Catholic influence, emigration out of the country and poor economic conditions have made establishment of autonomous churches difficult. There has been open opportunity for preaching, teaching and publicly proclaiming the gospel since World War II, but the traditions and problems in the country make Baptist advancement very slow and hard.

FRANCE

In 1810, a farmer in Flanders found a Bible hidden in an old house. For nearly ten years he and a small group studied it faithfully, forming a church in 1819. A young Scottish evangelist, Henri Pyt, spent a year and a half with them, teaching Baptist principles. After he left, the people printed and distributed information about their faith.

Howard Malcolm, a Baptist pastor from America, went to France for health reasons in 1831 and, seeing the great need and opportunities there, persuaded the American Baptists to enter the field. Casimir Rostan became the first Baptist missionary in France in 1832 with Ira Chase, a professor at Newton Theological Seminary (Institute), as the general director of the operation. Others followed, but political persecution made progress slow until after 1848.

By 1919, a French Baptist Union had been formed with about twenty-eight churches participating. Two world wars disrupted the work and destroyed many church buildings and internal struggles in the period between the wars further hindered advancement. Since 1945, when France was liberated from German occupation, the French Baptists have been free to resume their work, but a lack of internal unity and self-support have weakened organized Baptist work. Some American missionaries are involved there today, but reports indicate great struggle in achieving steady growth.

RUSSIA

To the twentieth century mind it is perhaps difficult to imagine that Russia could be or ever has been a bastion for the gospel and a stronghold of the Baptist faith. The gospel outreach actually rivaled the German Baptist movement in terms of successful growth. It is true, however, that the moral and ethical values that normally accompany the entrance of the gospel seemed to have little effect on the Russians.

The stage was set in Russia for the coming of the Baptists by the migration of Mennonite refugees from Prussia. The Russian empress, Catherine II, had given the assurance of freedom to those Mennonites fleeing conscription into military service in Germany. When they settled among the peasants in southern Russia, the Mennonites found a certain restlessness among the Russians. The end of the Crimean War had brought the granting of new freedoms, and they were open to evangelism.

The religious awakening saw not only a widespread witness by the Mennonites but a literature campaign in which the British and Foreign Bible Society distributed many copies of the Scriptures. Even the Russian Orthodox church clergy appreciated this work. Copies of the Scripture in hand, the restless peasants forsook the Orthodox church worship services and began attending Bible study groups called *stunden* (meaning "hours"). Out of this pietistic type of movement came a future leader of the Russian Baptists, Michael Ratushny.

While the Mennonites functioned in the Ukraine, a group of Molokans, who were much like Quakers, was active in the Russian state of Georgia. A German Baptist, Martin Kalweit, came to the area in 1862, and in time a Baptist church was established. One of the first converts was a young man, Basil Pavlov, who became a gifted preacher. After some years, Pavlov and Michael Ratushny met, and their respective groups united in 1884 to form the Russian Baptist Union.

Another convert to Baptist teaching was Ivan Prokhanov. He was well educated and began a Baptist periodical, *Beseda*, and later assembled a Russian hymnal for church use. He had, however, some difficulty with the rigid standards of the Baptists and never fully identified with the Russian Baptist movement, preferring to use the term "evangelical" instead.

The Russian government severely persecuted the Baptists, exiling some to Siberia and imprisoning others who sought to proselytize any from the Orthodox church. In spite of the hindrances, the Baptist numbers increased steadily until the Bolshevik Revolution. After the overthrow of the czarists, the new government granted some religious freedom, especially from state church harassment. Many Baptists had refused to fight in the Russian military during World War I, but they had shown willingness to serve in noncombat areas in the army, thus avoiding a serious conflict. According to Rushbrooke, there were nearly three million Baptists in Russia in the early 1920s.[7]

7. Torbet, *History of Baptists*, 183.

Political persecution was renewed in the 1920s because the atheistic Communist regime felt threatened by the presence of Baptists and other evangelicals. Religious education of children was outlawed, universal male conscription into the military was the order of the day, pastors were forbidden to vote, church leaders could not get food tickets (which were like a ration), religious organizations were assessed a special tax, parents were forbidden to teach their children at home, circulating Bibles was illegal and public church services were not allowed. When the revised constitution of the Union of Soviet Socialist Republics was adopted in 1936, religious freedom was guaranteed. It actually was interpreted, however, to mean only freedom of belief, and all the former restrictions were retained for the non-Orthodox.

The number of Baptists officially reported showed a marked decline by 1950. There had been a move in the 1940s to develop a somewhat ecumenical group called the Council of United Baptists, Evangelical Christians and Pentecostal Churches and Groups in the U.S.S.R. Thousands of Baptists (perhaps as many as 700,000) refused to join this government-sponsored group and apparently went underground because of its close link with the atheistic state leadership.

Since 1950 there have been numerous attempts to determine the size of the Baptist witness in Russia but with very little success. Today most church buildings belong to the state, the clergy are without salary and religious instruction is allowed only in closely-regulated worship services.

SUMMARY

Outside of the United States, Baptists have achieved success only in a few places; but the work has not been insignificant. The enthusiasm and zeal of the Great Commission to spread the gospel has kept the movement alive in the face of various forms and intensities of persecution. There are many new opportunities for evangelism and church planting open to new responders to the missionary calling. Oncken certainly set the tone for European Baptists with his belief that every Baptist was to be a missionary.

One thing stands out in the study of the European groups: that Baptist groups so often began with someone studying the Scriptures alone or in a small group. Through such a beginning they would come to Biblical belief regarding salvation, baptism and church organization and would subsequently learn of other Baptists somewhere who held to the same positions. One cannot underestimate the value and importance of the distribution of the Scriptures around the world.

9

Baptists in Conflict
1900-1950

One wonders if there can ever be honest denial of the fact of God. The "reasoning" savors of a guilty conscience rather than a genuine conviction. And then, what of the lurking fear that, after all, there may be a God?

An atheist said: There is one thing that mars all of the pleasure of my life. I am afraid that the Bible is true. If I could know of a certainty that death is an eternal sleep, I should be happy. But here is what pierces my soul—if the Bible is true I am lost forever.

—Unknown

The first fifty years of the twentieth century saw Baptists all over the world in serious conflict over important theological issues. As with any record of controversy, there is not a specific moment in time when forces just decide to confront one another; there is always a background that precipitated such a confrontation. Among Baptists this has been no exception.

The antecedents of what came to be known as the modernist-fundamentalist controversy go back in history to two major areas. The first was the philosophical approach called rationalism, and the second was the introduction of the theory of evolution. By the beginning of the twentieth century, both of these had entered into religious thought, found their way into colleges and seminaries and come to Baptist church pulpits and mission fields through the "new theology" that had been developed.

Rationalism is nearly as old as man's earthly existence. It involves acceptance of the absoluteness of reason and the rejection of faith and supernatural beliefs. When the serpent approached Eve in the Garden of Eden, his appeal for eating the forbidden fruit was that their minds would be more enlightened—". . . then your eyes shall be opened, and ye shall be as gods, *knowing* good and evil" (Gen. 3:5). The rational, reasoning mind is, therefore, something the human individual seeks to employ to his own personal satisfaction. The Greeks during the first millenium B.C. were avid rationalists, rejecting anything that was not clear to the human mind. The Romans followed with an extreme emphasis on the pragmatic—the only truth was what could be seen to *work* in the human world of utility. Later, the Renaissance took up the significance, importance and desire of human reason and achievement for the glory of man. A few hundred years later, the Enlightenment engulfed Western Europe, submitting everything to the power of man's intellect. Pierre Laplace (1749-1827) said:

> An intellect which at any given moment would know all the forces that animate nature and would know the mutual positions of the beings that compose nature—if this intellect were vast enough to submit its data to analysis—could condense into a single formula the movement of the greatest bodies of the universe and that of the lightest atom. *For such an intellect nothing could be uncertain*; and the future, like the past, would be present before its eyes.[1]

In the nineteenth century the idea of rationalism found its way into the realm of religion, subjecting many basic truths to the critical eye of human reason. The doctrines of Christianity came under the microscope of rational thought and were questioned if they did not receive the verification of reason. For

1. Leonard Krieger, *Kings and Philosophers*, 1689-1789 (New York: W. W. Norton and Company, 1970), 212.

many years the Biblical documents had been scrutinized, but in the nineteenth century the Mosaic authorship of the Pentateuch was "no longer a religious opinion" in most educated circles.[2] "The ordinary religious belief of educated persons has gradually ceased to include a six days' creation,"[3] accepting instead the idea of a gradual formation of the world. The basic doctrine of the resurrection of Christ was declared to be false. Instead, a mythical approach was developed that the disciples stole the body of Jesus for their own ambitious reasons, or that in the coolness of the tomb Jesus revived from a deep swoon and ever after could not convince His disciples that He was not a being from another world. Such are some of the rational criticisms of Christianity that were raised in the 1800s. From thousands of strands of thought, rationalistic thinkers began to replace the old and "obsolete" systems with new, vague and uncertain systems. Nineteenth century rationalism began in the German universities and seminaries, was transferred to the English-speaking colleges and seminaries and found its way into the minds and lives of some influential and learned Baptist leaders.

The second major contributor to the theological conflict was the evolutionary theory of Charles Darwin (1859) which was adopted by sociologists and given the name of social Darwinism. In this approach, the society is most important. Whatever is good for the society is good for the individual. In a way, the world can be made a better place to live, and mankind can and will become better and better. Social Darwinism, in other words, produces a form of humanly achieved millennialism. When this concept is brought into religious focus, it appears in the form of a Social Gospel with the emphasis on improvement of man's position in life rather than on the salvation of his soul from eternal hell.

Rationalism and the Social Gospel came together in religion, removing an authoritative Bible, questioning the reality of sin, doubting all supernatural elements of Christianity,

2. James Hastings, *Encyclopedia of Religion and Ethics*, vol. X (New York: Charles Scribner's Sons, 1922), 581.
3. Ibid.

making Jesus Christ nothing more than a noble example and identifying the task of religion as the preparation of a new world order which would become the kingdom of God. American Baptist champions of this cause were Shailer Mathews, Walter Rauschenbusch and Harry Emerson Fosdick.

Mathews attended Colby College and Newton Theological Institute before spending some years in Europe at the University of Berlin (1891), the largest university in Germany, well-known for its rationalist professors and the application of critical thinking. He subsequently became a professor at the University of Chicago Divinity School where he instilled his views in the minds of young and promising theologians. Rauschenbusch went to Westphalia, Germany, to study at the Gymnasium Guterstoh (a highly academic high school), took some work at the University of Berlin, returned to America to study at Rochester Seminary and later became professor of New Testament and Church History at Rochester. Harry Emerson Fosdick was prepared for the Baptist ministry at Colgate University and Union Theological Seminary, served as pastor of the First Presbyterian Church in New York City, taught practical theology at Union Theologial Seminary and pastored the independent Riverside Church in New York City. During his ministry among the Presbyterians, the Philadelphia presbytery sought to bring him to trial for his "modernistic" views which they termed as heresy. The General Assembly did not pass judgment on him, but it did ask him to conform to Presbyterian, conservative views or vacate his pulpit. He chose the latter alternative (1924) and took up the ministry at Riverside (1926).

With these modernist theologians (or, as they preferred, evangelical liberals) in prominent positions of influence on future Baptist leadership, it is not surprising that a movement to defend Baptist orthodoxy would come from earnest, theological conservatives (traditionalists). From this movement a new term was created—fundamentalist. The Baptist fundamentalists produced a series of volumes called The Fundamentals, emphasizing:

1. The inerrancy of the Bible
2. The deity of Christ

3. The virgin birth of Christ
4. The substitutionary atonement of Christ
5. The bodily resurrection of Christ
6. The imminent and personal return of Christ to establish His kingdom on earth

Approximately three million copies of the twelve paper-bound volumes were circulated among pastors and students between 1909 and 1915.

These diverse viewpoints among Baptists (and a similar situation was true among most denominational groups, but they are beyond the scope of this study) evoked emotional as well as intellectual participation, and the longer it continued, the deeper the entrenchment on each side. Rollin Hart wrote in *Forum* magazine:

> Two religions, so different that if one is true the other must be false, exist side by side within the confines of Protestantism. Had these two religions developed independently, no one would think for a moment of combining them.[4]

Modernists accepted the observable findings of science and used this new evidence in a reinterpretation of Christianity, even studying the Bible by the scientific method. The fundamentalists refused to accept the new findings of science, asserting that the Bible was to be taken as literal truth and authority in every aspect. The battlelines were now drawn for clashes on nearly every point of theology, and there was potential for long-range consequences that would rival those of medieval and Reformation proportions.

The Baptists in the American North were more involved in this conflict than those in the South. As discussed in chapter 4, the Baptist movement in the South was more Calvinistic and willing to give leadership power to a central, representative board or convention. The Northern Baptists, on the other hand, were more independent and opposed to organizational control. For this reason, plus the closer contact with Europe experienced by Baptists in the North, modernism took root north of the Mason-Dixon line.

4. Rollin Hart, *Forum*, November 1925.

Modernistic thinking entered some of the leading indepen-
dent Baptist churches in the Northeast late in the nineteenth
century. By 1905 it had reached leading churches in the
Midwest. Fountain Street Baptist Church in Grand Rapids,
Michigan, had had a long history of promotion of the gospel in
the area from 1837 to nearly 1900 and had established six
other Baptist churches in the growing city:
Second Baptist Church—1883
Wealthy Baptist Church—1886
Calvary Baptist Church—1889
Messiah Baptist Church (among the black population)—
  1889
Berean Baptist Church—1892
Scribner Baptist Church—1894
Lorence Asman of Asman Tract Publishers gleaned the fol-
lowing from sermons delivered at Fountain Street Baptist
Church by Pastor J. Herman Randall, demonstrating the influ-
ence of modernism in a local church.
February 5, 1905, discussing creation:

> The old theological conception that we have de-
> scribed, is gone forever, and men have come to
> think of the world not as being created any less by
> God, but they have come to think of God's method
> in the creation of the universe in the light of science,
> and the great evolutionary or nebular hypothesis.

March 5, 1905, discussing sin:

> So let me say, once for all, if any of us are perplexed
> by this teaching . . . of original sin, we need not feel
> that it is incumbent upon us to believe that in Adam
> the whole race fell. . . . This is a bit of theological fic-
> tion that has no basis in fact, and to which the in-
> telligent man can no longer give credance. . . . And
> so I thank God for the evolutionist. . . . I thank God
> that it is dispelling this old nightmare that has been
> resting on the human race for so many years. I hate
> that old idea of sin.

March 12, 1905, discussing salvation:

> Every man has to pay the penalties of his past sin.
> Salvation is the growing into this sweet and noble

and earnest and true and tender and honest manhood and womanhood in Jesus Christ.

March 19, 1905, discussing the Bible:

How different is this scientific doctrine from the ecclesiastical doctrine, and how much more satisfactory to the *rational mind* [italics mine]. The doctrine of
the church has been a horror. The end of the world
was coming . . . the wrath and the anger of God. The
scientific doctrine brings no dread and no horror.
. . . We have nothing to dread, nothing to fear.

May 14, 1905, discussing hell:

We all of us know that the popular conception of
hell has been of a literal place. . . . It has been the
most terrible of all the superstitions of the world. . . .
And I say very frankly for myself this morning, that I
am not such a craven coward as to worship a God
like that. If there is such a God, be he imaginary or
be he real, I will defy him through all eternity; and if
he wants to torture me eternally he can; but just as
long as I am consciously intelligent, such a being as
that can never, never conquer me.

An article in an August 24, 1906, issue of a Grand Rapids
newspaper regarded the calling of a new pastor, A. J. Wishart,
to Fountain Street. The article shows the modernist-fundamentalist conflict the church was experiencing:

The older members asked if Mr. Wishart was a
liberal preacher, intending to veto the call, but they
were silenced.

Mr. Randall ran an institutional church, preferring
ethical to biblical subjects for his sermons. One Sunday morning Col. Rose, now deceased, father of
Henry M. Rose, jumped to his feet in the midst of a
sermon, and shouted: "For the Lord's sake, Rev.
Randall, say one word for the Lord God Almighty."
"Just a moment, Col. Rose," Rev. Randall replied.
Col. Rose's spectacular request mirrored the sentiments of the older members of the congregation.

When the Northern Baptist Convention was formed in
1907, it did not provide much in the way of theological

framework for its members. They adopted no confession of faith because they wanted to preserve soul liberty and local church sovereignty. The declaration of the purpose of the new denomination was to provide a means of giving

> expression to the opinions of the constituency upon moral, religious and denominational matters, and to promote denominational unity and efficiency in efforts for the evangelization of the world.[5]

This broad, all-encompassing purpose allowed for a wide range of viewpoints, including the extreme elements of both modernism and fundamentalism. For this reason, the Northern Baptist Convention had an internal conflict much more extensive and acute than any other association of Baptists in the country. All other associations, though not exempt from the conflict, were more selective in screening their memberships.

About this same time, the interest in social problems and theological modernism, and a desire for interdenominational cooperation and unity, came together in the formation of the Federal Council of the Churches of Christ in America (today called the National Council). This council provided for cooperation among a wide variety of churches to apply the ethical principles of Christianity to the resolution of social problems. Their constitution was drawn up at a meeting in Carnegie Hall in New York in 1905, and thirty-three denominations accepted it at a meeting in Philadelphia in 1908. The Northern Baptist Convention has been a member of the Federal Council since the organization of the body in 1908.[6]

Promotion of these efforts to remedy social concerns, and the struggle between modernism and fundamentalism, became somewhat interrupted because of American involvement in World War I. A national effort toward preparation for and fighting of a war takes the major portion of both funds and energy. However, it did not stop the minds of religious leaders, and shortly after the war's end new ideas were added to the revived views of modernism.

Among Northern Baptists, a new program was launched. In

5. Torbet, *History of Baptists*, 438.
6. Ibid., 444.

1919 a report recommended to the convention meeting in Denver that a single budget should be raised to be divided among the various agencies of the convention, instead of each agency being supported individually. A general board of promotion, with its administrative committee made up of representatives from all convention agencies, was to be the agent to organize and carry out the fund raising. In 1920 thousands of Baptist "minute men and minute women" went to work to raise one hundred million dollars in five years. When the five-year program of this New World Movement was ended in 1924, its financial goal was only half attained. However, it had helped raise the level of contribution toward missions and schools, perhaps saving some from financial failure. The stimulus of the New World Movement did not last long, as evidence shows a rapid decline in funding for many years after 1926. The one major thing retained, however, was the concept of a unified budget for the comprehensive denominational support of missionary activity and schools.[7]

This unified budget, which was dispersed by the administrative arm of the convention, became another area of Baptist conflict. The sovereign local churches were giving money to a convention bureaucracy to distribute, but they had no say as to where the money was going. Missionaries were going to the fields with modernist views, which the fundamentalists could not accept. Several cases occurring between 1920 and 1936 are worthy of discussion.

Cecil G. Fielder was a missionary in Assam under the Northern Baptist Convention mission board. While in Assam, he wrote a lengthy confession of his faith and sent it to the mission board in New York. Among the things he stated were:
— Jesus definitely disclaims any intention of placing Himself on a level with God the Father.
— . . . every human being, no matter what his condition, is inalienably a child of God.
— The account of creation given in Genesis is wonderful. . . . I do not see how a finer explanation of our creation and our unhappy condition under sin could

7. Ibid., 392-394.

have been made than that. But now that we have the
theory of evolution, attested by so much convincing
evidence, I believe we have an explanation ever so
much more satisfying and joyous. . . .

— When we see ourselves in our true position as the
growing, erring children of God, is it not clear that
such a thing as an atonement, a making good, for us
by another could not possibly be acceptable to our
Father, or even considered by Him?

— . . . Vicarious sacrifice remains, but the atonement
cannot. It remains for us individually to make all
atonement we can for our past sins by living the kind
of life our Father yearns for.

— There is no man, no matter how vile, without some
solid good, some of the stuff of God, in him. There is
some invitation of God to which he will respond,
although he may have to hear it in the next world.[8]

The board of managers of the American Baptist Foreign
Mission Society met with Mr. Fielder, at the insistence of some
of the fundamentalists in the convention, and reviewed his
case. They recommended that Mr. Fielder take a year of theological study at Newton Theological Institute and that the
board would reconsider in 1926 the matter of his return to
Assam.

An additional concern arose among the fundamentalists
regarding a statement by Mr. Fielder in a personal letter to Dr.
R. T. Ketcham:

This has been my basic contention from the beginning, that I represent in general a goodly part of our
denomination, and that if such were the case I could
serve our denomination as a missionary in all good
conscience.

. . . The statement I wrote in Assam has been read
by many Baptists, persons of maturity and experience, mostly conservative in thinking, and, together with a fair presentation of the whole situa-

8. Robert T. Ketcham, *Facts for Baptists to Face* (Rochester, NY: Interstate
Evangelistic Association, 1936), 4-5.

tion, has gained their whole-souled expression of confidence in my fitness and right to serve as a missionary of our denomination. . . . One leading member of our denomination told me that he could not but be in favor of my return to Assam, since my point of view so closely paralleled his own.[9]

Needless to say, such revelations caused distress and even deeper conflict. Rumors and charges of modernism were met by convention leaders denying that such views were held. The fundamentalists who spoke out against modernism were charged with "mutiny," and were called "falsifiers," "destructionists"and "religious bolshevists."[10] The fact of the encroachment of modernism into the Northern Baptist Convention became more evident as time progressed.

In the case of a Mr. Randle, missionary to China, another aspect of modernism appeared. Dr. W. B. Riley was explaining at a Milwaukee convention meeting the charge that Randle refused to accept the deity of Christ. Dr. Franklin, the moderator, stopped him and indicated that he had a letter from Mr. Randle. Waving it in the air, he said, "God Almighty answered Dr. Riley by mail this morning." He then read the letter disproving the charge, and Dr. Riley left the platform amidst hoots and jeers from the audience. It became known later that while Dr. Franklin was reading one letter to the audience, he had in his pocket another letter from Mr. Randle addressed to the board of managers, which stated:

I am also accused of being unwilling to answer in the affirmative the question, "Do you believe that Christ is God?" This was a prayer meeting which I was leading and not a class in theology. Nor was it quite the proper time or place to catechize the leader because he had not expressed his faith in the phraseology which certain individuals were accustomed to use. However, to be perfectly fair to all parties concerned, I must say that I do not wish to ascribe to Jesus any higher position than that which

9. Ibid.
10. Ibid., 7.

he claimed for himself. He did not claim to be God,
but he did say that he was the Son of God. I was not
asked as to my faith in the divinity of Jesus, the deity
of Jesus, or his place in the Trinity. I was asked to
answer categorically whether Jesus was God. Passages like the following make an affirmative answer
to that question rather difficult. 1 Tim. 2:15; Matt.
27:46; Jno. 23:46(?); Col. 3:1; Luke 9:48; Matt. 3:17;
Matt. 17:17; Luke 10:22.[11]

These cases led to conflict over the foreign board expense
accounts, allocation of missionary dollars, designated gifts,
missionary schools, publications, youth material and educational institutions. The following, some random samples from
Dr. Ketcham's book *Facts for Baptists to Face* (1936), will illustrate
the various situations of dispute.

Myron J. Hertel was a 1936 graduate of Andover-Newton
Seminary and ordained by the Boston East Association. In
answer to ordaining questions, he said:

The death of Christ on the cross is only an example
of a man dying for his own convictions. . . . The
blood of Jesus was of no more value in the saving of
a soul than the water in which Pilate washed his
hands.

During the executive session of the ordination council, one
of Mr. Hertel's classmates, speaking in his behalf, said:

Mr. Hertel is a fine fellow. I have been to dances
with him and he has never lost his purity. We have
attended card parties and he has never been dishon-
est or lost his temper.

Dr. A. S. Hobart of Crozer Seminary wrote a book entitled
Transplanted Truth from Romans in which he states on page 29:

I cannot see anything understandable or acceptable
in the theory that my guilt and my penalty were
placed upon Christ, or that Christ's holiness is im-
parted to me, in any way that involves a substitution
of His holiness for mine or His suffering for what was
due me, that view of the theory of the atonement

11. Ibid., 8.

finds no foothold in my consciousness or my reason.

Furthermore, Professor H. C. Vedder of Crozer Seminary, the often quoted writer of the *Short History of the Baptists*, said:

> Of all the slanders men have perpetrated against the Most High, this is positively the most impudent, the most insulting. No, sin cannot be escaped by a bloody sacrifice. Jesus never taught and never authorized anybody to teach in His name that "He suffered in our stead, and bore the penalty for our sins."

The fundamentalists within the Northern Baptist Convention could not agree with such points as these, so in 1923 they organized within the convention, becoming the Baptist Bible Union. The organizational meeting was held in a large tent in Kansas City, Missouri. Individual personality conflicts developed among the fundamentalists in the union and served as a foreshadowing of the significant fragmentation to come. R. E. Neighbor, who originated the idea of a union of fundamentalists, J. Frank Norris, T. T. Shields, A. C. Dixon, R. T. Ketcham and W. B. Riley, among others, played prominent roles. Norris, Shields and Dixon skillfully maneuvered Neighbor out of any position in the leadership of the union, and Dixon soon lost interest, leaving Norris and Shields in strong leadership roles. Later Riley broke with Norris over some personal matters and lost interest, while Ketcham sought to serve as a catalyst in the group.

The union drew up a confession of faith, which was essentially the old New Hampshire Confession with the addition of a premillennial clause. Membership was on an individual, not church, basis. Anyone who signed a card indicating acceptance of the confession of faith was admitted to membership. Such an arrangement allowed for a wide variety of people to participate, some of whom were quite irresponsible, others not very successful in the ministry, which caused the union some embarrassment.

The union, in spite of all its limitations, provided a platform from which fundamentalists could deliver a militant defense of the historic Baptist faith against the rapidly rising modernism.

They held preconvention meetings and planned strategy for the coming convention sessions but, as Dr. Ketcham later wrote in an article sent to his friend, Art Fetzer, "We never won a single battle on any issue."

In 1931, Des Moines (Iowa) University, which the fundamentalist arm through the Baptist Bible Union operated, completely broke down. In personal material shared with this author, Dr. Ketcham recounted that:

A slander started on Dr. Shields (the University president) and his secretary. [The slander] claimed that they stayed together in a hotel room in Hotel Des Moines. I know this was not true because I was at the train to meet him when he came into Des Moines at 8:30 the next morning from Chicago. But like all slanders, it grew, and the result was that the students took over and broke the place up— smashed everything in the place and some of the Board of Trustees had to hide in places in the building to keep from being hit by bricks and rotten eggs and all of this.

At the meeting of the union in May 1932, only about thirty members were present, and the Baptist Bible Union was ended.

Open conflict had developed on the floors of several annual meetings of the Northern Baptist Convention, but the 1928 meeting in Chicago illustrates the extent to which the struggles had gone. Dr. Ketcham recounted in personal information shared with this author a long story, which is condensed here. The fundamentalist group had been defeated in convention sessions over and over again. Ketcham felt that the battle could not be won and asked Dr. Riley to leave the convention with him.

One of the problems at this point was that the salaried or paid employees of the convention were quite large in number and were also serving as delegates to the convention meetings. These paid employees always voted nearly unanimously for anything the convention leadership wanted. Therefore, Riley felt that if a motion could be put through to disfranchise all the employees, the fundamentalist segment could defeat the modernist group. Ketcham responded, "How are you going to do that? Should you put up a resolution to disfranchise the salaried servants, they would not be disfranchised yet until that passed. Do you think they are going to sit there and let us pass it?"

In 1928, a few hundred fundamentalist pastors met to discuss how to influence the election of convention officers to be held the following morning. They concluded that many of the nominees on the sample ballot were modernistic to some degree. It was agreed that the fundamentalists should put out a whole new slate of nominees sharing their views, present the nominations in addition to those already nominated, and let the people choose from either list.

In order to have such a ballot prepared by 9:00 A.M., it was necessary to find a printer to do it during the night. The police were asked if they knew of any printing places they had seen open on their night patrols, and one was located. The ballots were at the convention hall by 9:00 A.M. and the nominees were presented to the delegates. But when the vote was tabulated, the modernist group had defeated the fundamentalists by approximately two to one.

Several fundamentalist pastors, with their churches, left the Northern Baptist Convention. This in turn brought another series of conflicts over ownership of church property. If a congregation voted by simple majority or more (at least fulfilling the requirements of its own bylaws) to withdraw from the fellowship of the convention, did not that majority retain the title to and use of the church property? One of the most classic cases, from Princeton, Indiana, will serve as an example of this type of struggle, although there were many more.

At a constitutionally called and conducted business meeting of the First Baptist Church in Princeton, Indiana, the congregation voted ninety-eight to eighteen to withdraw from fellowship with the Evansville Baptist Association, the Indiana Baptist Convention and the Northern Baptist Convention. Their stated reasons dealt with modernism and tendencies toward Communism, which they believed were found in many areas of denominational work. After numerous maneuverings by the minority group, the case reached the civil courts to settle the dispute over property title and use on January 16, 1939. Deliberations lasted two and one-half days. Church documents from the time the church began in 1894 were evaluated, and the minority's key witnesses were called to take the stand on behalf of the convention. Testimony and cross-examinations revealed many irregular and non baptistic views on the part of the convention witnesses. As an example, the following part of the questioning by the church's attorney and the responses of Dr. T. J. Parsons, executive secretary of the Indiana Baptist Convention, included:

> Question: If one single member of that church voted against withdrawing from the Convention, that one person would be the true church in your judgment?
>
> Parsons: That is not a proper question in my judgment.
>
> Question: The court rules on whether a question is proper or not, Doctor.
>
> Parsons: We would recognize that one member can defend his rights.
>
> Question: And he would be the church?
>
> Parsons: Yes, because he did not go out.

Further testimony from pastors and denominational leaders departed from accepted Baptist polity, leading the court to dismiss the case in favor of the majority. One appeal was made, with the result that the judge issued a permanent injunction against the minority.[12]

This type of action went on in numerous church situations across America, with differing results—sometimes the convention minority would win, sometimes the voting majority would win. The Baptist witness was harmed as a result, and the growth of the movement was hindered in much of the North.

During all of these conflicts there were those who, to varying degrees, believed they should leave the convention, whatever the cost. The Biblical base from which the separatist fundamentalists worked was Amos 3:3, 2 Corinthians 6:14—7:1 and Ephesians 5:11. They also had the earlier testimony of

---

12. Robert T. Ketcham, "The Princeton Case," Baptist Bulletin, May 1940, 2-11.

Charles Haddon Spurgeon and his example of separation from that which he considered nonbiblical. (See page 99.)

As we have noted before, there are always key men who come to positions of prominence and leadership during times of crisis. Four of these men have been chosen for this record because of their involvement in wide-reaching new movements among Baptists. Each of these took the separatist position and began new Baptist associational fellowships or denominations outside of the Northern Baptist Convention.

1. Dr. T. T. Shields led in the organizing of the Regular Baptist Missionary and Educational Society in Canada (1927). At first it was a movement within the Canadian Baptist Convention, but later it became completely separate.

2. Dr. R. T. Ketcham led in the formation of the General Association of Regular Baptist Churches (1932). It became an association of only those churches that had severed all relations with the Northern Baptist Convention.

3. Dr. W. B. Riley was the leading proponent of the Conservative Baptist Fellowship (1947). This organization allowed members to retain relationships in the Northern Baptist Convention. Individuals and churches established a mission board to ensure fundamental missionaries on the fields of the world.

4. Dr. J. Frank Norris provided the main impetus for the formation of the Baptist Bible Fellowship (1950), which consisted of individual and corporate churches that wished to join it to complete separation from the Northern Baptist Convention.

Many other state and local separatist Baptist associations formed, but these four achieved national stature and to some extent absorbed many of the local associations.

All of this tremendous conflict, as well as their militancy against the scientific and modernistic ideas, earned the Baptists in the North a reputation of "fighting Baptists." The court suits brought by the various segments of the Northern Baptist Convention also contributed to this new reputation.

In an article in the *Baptist Bulletin*, G. H. Moulds summarized the theological viewpoints of the modernist-fundamentalist conflict in a series of comparisons:

The Modernists tended to say: The Bible contains the Word of God; and in the original is open to criticism like any other document. The Bible is inspiring.

The Fundamentalists tended to say: The Bible is the Word of God; and in the original is inerrant and hence beyond criticism. The Bible is verbally inspired.

The Modernists tended to say: The God-enlightened individual reason or the voice of the living Church is the means of reaching truth.

The Fundamentalists tended to say: It is necessary that there be some kind of an authoritative, inspired, written record given by God to man: The Bible has demonstrated itself to be such, and hence worthy of every trust; it is the basis for our reasoning.

The Modernists tended to say: Biblical material has value only as it proves that value in use.

The Fundamentalists tended to say: The Bible is of value primarily because it is true.

The Modernists tended to say: God is immanent in all men. The religious liberty of the individual soul is of prime importance.

The Fundamentalists tended to say: God is transcendent, over the universe. The individual's obedience to God's will is of prime importance.

The Modernists tended to say: Christianity, as all else, is of natural origin and evolutionary.

The Fundamentalists tended to say: Christianity is of supernatural origin and static in its essentials.

The Modernists tended to say: Salvation is through the moral influence of the Cross and by following Jesus' leadership.

The Fundamentalists tended to say: Salvation is by Christ's substitutionary sacrifice, and through His blood shed on the Cross.

The Modernists tended to say: Jesus was a son of God.

The Fundamentalists tended to say: Jesus was and is God.

The Modernists tended to say: God is the Father of all; and all men are brothers.

The Fundamentalists tended to say: God is the Father of only such as are born again; men are really only brothers in Christ.

The Modernists tended to say: There is a unity underlying all things: God is all and in all.

The Fundamentalists tended to say: There is a dualistic paradox underlying all things: God and the Devil; righteousness and sin; Heaven and Hell.

The Modernists tended to say: Religious knowledge is acquired through discovery, just as any other form of knowledge.

The Fundamentalists tended to say: Religious truth is divinely given by revelation.[13]

As is often true in conflicts, the major issue expands until nearly every known area of difference becomes fair game for open conflict and destruction of fellowship. The modernists were content to work gradually to achieve their goals with a minimum of emotional emphasis. The fundamentalists, on the other hand, were aggressive, defensive, offensive and emotional as they sought to purge the modernistic views out of the convention.

Ultimately, the fundamentalists came to realize the futility of trying to ``clean up'' the convention and withdrew fellowship from it. New and spirited groups were begun among the Baptists in the North, and their zeal produced rapid expansion, growth and outreach.

Changes in the times after 1950 would lead to severe

13. G. H. Moulds, ``The Conflict between the Modernists and the Fundamentalists in the Northern Baptist Convention since 1920,'' Baptist Bulletin, January 1941, 3-4.

fragmentation of Baptists over issues that in the past would not have been a problem.

> The duty of Christians in times of apostasy and seducement is to contend for the faith once given to the saints. Truth is honored by bold and resolute defense of it. There is not only a time to show love, but there is a time to show valor. To be valiant for the truth is to defend it in the time of opposition, and to fight for it as believers, knowing that there is no other way in the pursuit of faith and freedom.
>
> "If the foundations be destroyed, what can the righteous do?"
>
> —John E. Millheim

10
Baptists in Fragmentation
1950-1980

This know also, that in the last days perilous times shall come.

For men shall be lovers of their own selves, covetous, boasters, proud, blasphemers, disobedient to parents, unthankful, unholy,

Without natural affection, trucebreakers, false accusers, incontinent, fierce, despisers of those that are good,

Traitors, heady, highminded, lovers of pleasures more than lovers of God;

Having a form of godliness, but denying the power thereof: from such turn away.

For of this sort are they which creep into houses, and lead captive silly women laden with sins, led away with divers lusts,

Ever learning, and never able to come to the knowledge of the truth.

—2 Timothy 3:1-7

Likewise also these filthy dreamers defile the flesh, despise dominion, and speak evil of dignities.

These are spots in your feasts of charity, when they feast without you, feeding themselves without fear: clouds they are without water, carried about of winds; trees whose fruit withereth, without fruit, twice dead, plucked up by the roots;

Raging waves of the sea, foaming out their own shame; wandering stars, to whom is reserved the blackness of darkness for ever.

These are murmurers, complainers, walking after their own lusts; and their mouth speaketh great swelling words, having men's persons in admiration because of advantage.

But, beloved, remember ye the words which were spoken before of the apostles of our Lord Jesus Christ;

How that they told you there should be mockers in the last time, who should walk after their own ungodly lusts.

These be they who separate themselves, sensual, having not the Spirit.

But ye, beloved, building up yourselves on your most holy faith, praying in the Holy Ghost,

Keep yourselves in the love of God, looking for the mercy of our Lord Jesus Christ unto eternal life.

And of some have compassion, making a difference:

And others save with fear, pulling them out of the fire; hating even the garment spotted by the flesh. Now unto him that is able to keep you from falling, and to present you faultless before the presense of his glory with exceeding joy,

To the only wise God our Saviour, be glory and majesty, dominion and power, both now and ever. Amen.

—Jude 8, 12, 13, and 16-25

The decades following 1950 were extremely complicated. Advances in science, technology, communications and power for destruction expanded to limits previously unknown. There are several major aspects to explore before making any judgments about the Baptists in this period: politics, economics, social aspects, education and religion.

THE POLITICAL ASPECT

World War II came to a close quickly after the implementation of the first atomic bombs. Man's power to destroy had been increased thousands of times. People were filled with fear, distrust, tension and suspicion as they attempted to cope with the new positive and negative forces. Political leaders scrambled to find ways to end wars or at least decrease man's inhumanity to man.

The war's end saw a world carved into three basic parts: an Eastern, Communist world; a Western, free world; and a neutral world which was to become fair game for both East and West, as each sought to strengthen its position in the world. An attempt to assure the harmonious coexistence between Communism and free enterprise was made through the formation of the United Nations in June 1945. Structured to give representation to all legally established governments, the United Nations brought together people of many different political and economic philosophies. Although never publicly stated, membership in the U.N. actually meant giving up some rights of national sovereignty in exchange for participation in an international peace-keeping military force, which would police disturbances around the world. Multinational armed forces would be under the command of U.N. designated people. And the Communist and free worlds clashed in Korea in the 1950s, Vietnam in the 1960s and the Near East in the 1970s.

The goal of the U.N. was to produce a one-world political system that would reduce the threats and fears of the world. If Alexander the Great or the Roman Caesars could have seen this system for one-world government, they would have rejoiced, for in their respective eras they had sought a similar goal with temporary success.

The U.N., however, was not able to accomplish the goal of peace in the world. Instead of peace, the world experienced the Cold War as East and West stared at and threatened each other across iron and bamboo curtains. International tensions and extensive nuclear testings sent frightened people in the 1950s to the construction of fallout shelters.

In the American government, a strong emphasis was placed on searching out Communists in America. Senator Joseph McCarthy led the investigation in the Senate, while the House Committee on Un-American Activities served a similar role in the House of Representatives. Thousands of pages of testimony and exhibits were entered into the *Congressional Record* of the 1950s regarding accusations of people as Communists or Communist sympathizers. Organizations, both secular and religious, were labeled as Communist Front Organizations if they espoused any Communist ideologies but were not active members of the Communist Party. The Federal Bureau of Investigation played an active role in searching out those suspected of un-American actions.

October 4, 1957, marks the beginning of another form of political tension—the Russians sent the first artificial satellite into space. A whole new frontier was opened, and the space race was on. Manned space flights, a walk on the moon, exploration of distant planets and observation of activities all over the world were now possible.

Nuclear arms control negotiations continued endlessly while nuclear warheads mounted on rockets were deployed strategically around the globe. Even a "hotline" telephone system between the offices of the president of the United States and the Russian premier was installed. And yet, with all the talks and promises of world peace, military personnel continued to die in conflict areas around the world or were held hostage in foreign lands.

Radicalism became the order of the day. Protest marches were carried out in behalf of civil rights for blacks, women and underprivileged people of all races and nationalities. College campuses became scenes of activism and confrontation between armed police or militia and rioting students. Berkeley and Kent State were notable examples.

These uncertain, uncontrollable political struggles magnified the restlessness, doubt and questioning of values. Brainwashing of American personnel in North Korean prison camps became possible because of the erosion of traditional values that had marked American uniqueness from its very beginning.

THE ECONOMIC ASPECT

Historians and economists generally agree that the Great Depression ended because of the markets created by the outbreak of war in Europe in 1939. During World War II, world productivity was phenomenal, even though governmental restrictions kept wages and prices under strict control.

In the United States, wage and price controls were lifted during the Eisenhower administration, and an inflationary spiral began. With wage increases becoming practically automatic year after year, employees were able to purchase consumer products on credit, certain that next year their pay would be even higher. For nearly thirty years affluency marked many families in this country and abroad. Not only needs but wants were fulfilled for many, creating an enlarging gap between the "haves" and the "have nots." This gap was viewed with little concern and compassion by the affluent. Those who found it hard to maintain even subsistence living were preyed upon by left-wing economists, who promoted some form of socialist system. Nation after nation moved to dependence upon government, not just for protection but for economic support. For the affluent, there was little need for God—for the poor, government became the savior.

Tensions between management and labor changed the structure of the industrial system. Small shops could not compete with the ever-increasing conglomerate corporations, and the personal relationships between the manufacturer, merchant and consumer were lost to the business world. Pride of product deteriorated into mass production of lower quality merchandise.

Transportation between 1950 and 1980 went from railroads to giant trucking units, from droning propeller planes to streaking jets, and automobiles sped faster and faster on winding superhighways. Products and people could now be moved internationally with tremendous speed. Traveling anywhere became a matter of hours instead of days. The shrinking world brought many people into contact with other cultures, which were exploited for personal or corporate gain. Need for fuel ripped jungles apart and destroyed villages and cultures. Man's inhumanity to man and nature increased with the lust for wealth.

In many nations, especially those of the so-called Third World, political upheaval was accompanied by economic breakdown. These factors especially changed the face of missions as the costs rose rapidly, and churches came under the financial stress of highly increased budgets.

THE SOCIAL ASPECT

Perhaps the actual frustration among the people was acted out most on the social scene. The spirit of the age was one of abandonment of restraints.

By the 1950s most families had television, and the influence of TV on the average person was tremendous. As Francis Schaeffer points out in *How Should We Then Live?*, the selection of camera position accompanied by certain voice inflections became a slanted medium for coverage of information.[1] The viewer saw the tremendous devastation of a riot, only to discover that in reality the coverage was at a single building or intersection. The power of the media increased, and changes in journalistic purpose and style brought about trial by media, making trial by law more difficult.

Television also produced some informative material that could not have been realized before—the coronation of Queen Elizabeth II of England, the inauguration of American presidents, the royal wedding of Prince Charles and Lady Diana. Culture, information and interpretation of events around the world were brought into the average living room.

One less positive factor of televison's influence was in the development of an entertainment-demanding people. The result was that people were becoming observers rather than participants and dependents rather than creators. Serious implications for the churches sprang from this attitude.

In the 1960s, another social contributor began to operate—the counterculture. Disenchanted with what they saw in the established, traditional institutions of society, many young people turned to nonconformity, rebellion against the "establishment," advocation of free love and security in communal living. Moving to what was thought to be a new freedom, many discovered themselves under a new form of bondage. T. Walter Walbank summarizes this movement:

> The counterculture calls for a "new morality" whose
> fundamental tenets reject the concept of original sin.
> Instead, it sees human nature as basically good but

1. Francis Schaeffer, *How Should We Then Live?* (Old Tappan, NJ: Fleming H. Revell Company, 1976), 239-241.

thwarted by oppressive institutions. In its emphasis on liberating the spirit, it recalls in different degrees both Rousseau's "noble savage" and nineteenth century Marxism, as well as the "life, liberty, and the pursuit of happiness" of the Declaration of Independence. There is thus a strong tendency to reject authority and what is regarded as institutional manipulation. This rejection is accompanied by an insistence to follow personal modes of conduct, as expressed in the cliché "Do your own thing."[2]

Disenchantment of this magnitude led to wide use of alcohol and drugs, a turning to the occult and the language of futility found in the lyrics of rock music. The youth followed the permissiveness of Dr. Spock, the philosophy of Herbert Marcuse, the psychology of Erich Fromm and the methodology of Marshall McLuhan. Fashion, politics, the arts, work habits and personal excesses horrified parents and the established institutions. And instead of assuming some responsibility and working to resolve the problems, the youth blamed a nebulous "environment."

Perhaps the most subtle influence of all came in the form of secular humanism, which places man instead of God at the center of everything. The ideal was the true Renaissance man, who had ability and the opportunity to make his world a better place. Human achievement became the god of the age. It continued the notion of the Social Gospel with its deliberate emphasis on man's improvement. So appealing did this philosophy seem that it invaded every segment of society, including religion, where man made his own gods rather than served the Lord God.

THE EDUCATIONAL ASPECT

After "sputnik," the educational world panicked and rushed into many crash programs of curriculum revision. The reasoning was the Russians had to have a superior educational

---

2. T. Walter Wallbank, et al., *Civilization Past and Present* (Glenview, IL: Scott, Foresman and Company, 1971), 808.

system or they would not have been first in space. The Europeans could speak several languages while many Americans were struggling with their native tongue. Educational programs expanded, allowing students various tracks or options to select that which seemed best for them.

Schools soon began to take up functions previously handled by the family. Hot lunch programs, counseling services, sex education classes and a multiplicity of time-consuming extracurricular activities became the norm for the student. Along with these came the increased questioning of traditional values. The courts declared that proscribed prayers were illegal in public schools. Instead of the traditional absolutes, a new system of relative ethics was introduced, because some believed that schools should not teach values at all. The non-value became a new value.

THE RELIGIOUS ASPECT

By 1950, the modernism of the first half of the twentieth century had been given a new name—liberalism. It continued to champion the Social Gospel and brotherly love and included a wide range of theological viewpoints. The National and World Councils of Churches incorporated this ecumenical spirit into their organizational structures, as any list of the denominational affiliates will demonstrate. Among those active in these liberal-oriented organizations were some apparent Communist Party members and others who were sympathetic to Communism.

In an effort to counter the liberal councils, the fundamentalist American Council of Christian Churches was organized in 1941. In 1948, the fundamentalists convened in Amsterdam to form the International Council of Christian Churches. The struggle between liberalism and fundamentalism had now become worldwide, and the scope of the struggle began to include more than theology. Sides were chosen on political matters, as illustrated by the World Council's support of mainland China's Communist-dominated position and the International Council's support of General Chiang Kai-shek's Chinese government in exile on Taiwan.

The two sides also collided over the influence and inclusion of Communists or alleged Communists in the religious organization. American and International Council members joined the government in identifying Communists in the religious world. Pages of testimony and exhibits address these matters in the *Congressional Record* of the middle 1950s. Besides government documentation, groups published lists of "Pink Fringe" organizations, which were believed to be sympathetic to Communism in the mainline denominations.

For the most part, the media linked the anticommunists and fundamentalists together and were quick to suggest their militant vindictiveness. A subtle attack came from the press when they referred to the House Committee on Un-American Activities as the House Un-American Activities Committee. While the fundamentalists were either ignored by the press or scoffed at as "fighting fundamentalists," the liberals received favorable press which ignored their equally militant spirit.

A Baptist pastor, Dr. Archer Weniger, who was also the chairman of the Board of Trustees of the San Francisco Conservative Baptist Theological Seminary, attended the meeting of the General Assembly of the National Council of Churches in San Francisco in 1960. He published a report on the meeting, entitled *Ecumenical Folly*, in which he described those members present.

> This was the largest collection of heretics, modernists, pinks, scoffers, higher critics, false prophets, and religious subversives in the triennium. . . .[3]

He recorded a number of participating, prominent personalities of various faiths: Dr. James Pike (Episcopalian bishop), Dr. Theo. Gill (*Christian Century* magazine), Dr. Henry Van Dusen (Union Theological Seminary), Dr. Truman Douglass (United Church of Christ) and Dr. Edwin Dahlberg (Baptist, retiring president of the National Council of Churches).

Dr. Pike took over as the leading spokesman for liberalism, succeeding Dr. Harry Emerson Fosdick. *Ecumenical Folly* reveals

---

3. G. Archer Weniger, *Ecumenical Folly* (Wheaton, IL: Sword of the Lord Foundation, 1961), 3.

Dr. Pike's attitude toward anticommunists in a quote from the *Pacific Churchman*:

> Only God can judge whether these individuals [anti-communists] are headed for hell; but that they are its servants in this present situation is perfectly evident.[4]

There were some who tried to soften the continued conflict between the extremes of liberalism and fundamentalism. The advocates of the new theology, or *neoorthodoxy*, claimed to be opposed to liberalism as such, but their viewpoint tended to be the old modernism presented in a more acceptable language. While liberalism rejected the verbal plenary inspiration of the Bible, the neoorthodox founder, Karl Barth, claimed to believe in inspiration. However, his idea of inspiration was not that the text itself was inspired by God, but that the Bible was inspired when it inspired the reader. The inspiration of the Bible was determined on the basis of the individual's response to it. By and large, then, the Bible had no real, significant difference or greater finality of authority than any other book. This concept caused theological divisions of liberals, neoorthodox and fundamentalists.

Later, the March 1956 issue of *Christian Life* magazine carried an editorial introducing another concept. While neoorthodoxy was an attempt to soften liberalism, this *new evangelicalism* was designed to soften the fundamentalist end of the conflict. The editorial, entitled "Is Evangelical Theology Changing?", indicated that the new evangelicals would attempt:

1. A more friendly attitude toward science
2. A willingness to reexamine the inspiration of the Bible in the light of science, philosophy and neoorthodoxy
3. An increased emphasis on scholarship
4. A greater willingness on the part of evangelical theologians to converse with liberal theologians

This latest concept divided the religious world into liberals, neoorthodox, new evangelicals and fundamentalists. Baptist churches, like most other denominations, were forced to take a position somewhere among these choices.

4. Ibid., 15.

One further theological concept was introduced into the field of evangelism. For want of better terminology, it became known as "easy believism." Men such as D. L. Moody and Charles Finney in the nineteenth century, Billy Sunday in the 1920s and Oscar Lowrey in the 1930s had led massive evangelism campaigns. The theme was explicitly the gospel of Christ but placed an emphasis on the Christian's responsibility after conversion. The Lordship of Christ was highly emphasized with its accompanying belief of a changed life as evidence of salvation. As the Great Depression became more firmly entrenched, and the second world war was fought, such massive campaigns became improper and, in some areas, illegal. Following the war, however, a new kind of evangelism was born. Gigantic campaigns were held in the major metropolitan areas of America and spread nearly around the globe. These campaigns were ecumenical in nature, having organizational committees composed of Roman Catholics, liberal Protestants, new evangelicals and some fundamentalists.

These modern evangelistic services stressed "accepting Christ" or "believing in Jesus." If one came to Christ, it was implied, all his problems would be solved. The finest of gospel music was used in the services, the best psychological motivators were used in promotion, and the preaching was of the simple gospel message. After nearly thirty years of modernistic emphasis on reason over faith, and fundamentalist attempts to preserve the Biblical faith, thousands of people flocked to the meetings. For the most part, the messages were the same in theme and goal; only the Biblical starting place and story were different. Personal workers led those responding to the invitation to the Scripture for salvation assurance. Each individual was then encouraged to pray—in his own words and in his own way.

There was one problem, however: the whole truth was not used. Responders learned about faith unto salvation and accepted that, but they were not informed of the Lordship of Christ in their lives. Because the cosponsors of the campaigns held such diverse theologies, the responders were encouraged to join "the church of your choice." They were not given much, if any, instruction on how to locate a Bible-believing church.

Thus, many returned to liberal churches where the gospel was not preached.

Because of this lack of steering people into fundamental churches, and the link with liberals and Roman Catholics, many fundamentalists grew disenchanted with the popular evangelism and chose not to support such campaigns. Whereas the fundamentalists had separated from the modernists in the 1920s and 1930s, now they were faced with separation from gospel-preaching people who chose not to separate from liberals. Thus a second degree of separation came into the religious ranks. Later there would come a third degree of separation: fundamentalists from other fundamentalists who chose to fellowship with those who fellowshiped with liberals. The following diagram illustrates the degrees of separation:

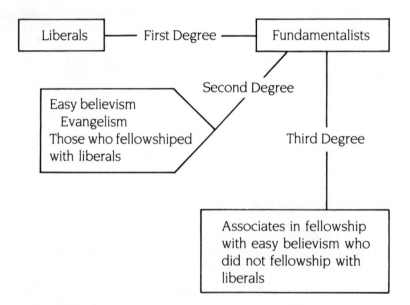

During the late 1960s many conferences were held in local churches at which invitations were given to accept the Lordship of Christ. Hundreds responded to these invitations. These conferences drew some criticism because they appeared to border on the holiness view of a second work of grace, whereby the believer some time after salvation receives the Holy Spirit. An analysis of the respondents, however, revealed that most of them had become Christians under easy believism and were now seeing for the first time the need of Christ's Lordship. In a way it was reminiscent of Acts 19:2, where the converts at Ephesus had not heard anything about the Holy Spirit.

A complication in separation came when local ministerial associations, made up of the pastors of the older, established denominations, were formed for fellowship, promotion of social challenges and enhancement of community brotherhood. Many of these men were loyal to the National and World Councils of Churches and followed the programs and decisions of their officials. A Comity Program was established in some areas to control the location of new church buildings. The local ministerial groups would work with city planners regarding zoning and church construction. The large area was to be divided into territorial sections, and in each section a church of a different faith would be constructed—a Methodist church here, a Baptist church there, a Roman Catholic church in another, and so on. In the ecumenical spirit, the people were to be encouraged—nearly required—to attend the church located in their district of residence. The ministerial groups would have the say about which churches would be allowed. One can imagine the lack of success of any fundamentalist church in receiving a building permit. The plan was approved, but in no location was it ever carried out successfully.

A word must be included regarding the influence of radio and television on the religious world. Before 1950, opportunities had been available for Christian radio broadcasting, but the rates had been somewhat prohibitive. After 1950, rates were lowered because of competition, and many local churches chose to enter the field of broadcasting. Because of the increasing demand for entertainment, some religious broadcasting turned to showmanship, glamour and enhancing production techniques. Hundreds of religious broadcasts became national and international, and later many entered the television medium. To finance these ever-widening ventures, it became necessary to turn to Christians everywhere for contributions, and gimmicks were often used for enticement. For some Christians, these broadcasts became a substitute for their local churches, and the "electronic church" was thus created.

THE BAPTIST RESPONSES

Baptists had a choice of many possible responses to the rapid and dynamic changes of this technological age. The Baptist position on local church sovereignty allowed for more responses than were possible in episcopalian or presbyterian forms of church government. Local Baptist churches and associations took on local color, reflecting the indigenous principle. Technically, all the decisions were some variation of one of the following:

1. Accept the external and internal pressures and yield completely to the dominant forces of liberalism.
2. Take some form of moderate, compromising position in an attempt to satisfy the demands of both liberalism and fundamentalism.
3. Accept the fundamentalist position on theological and practical matters, and separate completely from liberalism and those who fellowship with liberals.

The American Baptist Convention leadership basically chose to follow the liberalism with which the National and World Councils were identified. The convention had held membership in and actively supported these two organizations from their birth. Dr. Edwin Dahlberg, a convention Baptist, served as president of the National Council for a time. It would, however, be unfair as well as incorrect to say that every American Baptist Convention church was primarily liberal, for many continued to use their local church sovereignty and autonomy and continued preaching the gospel of Christ as Baptists historically had done.

The structure of the convention, however, made support of the denominational programs nearly mandatory for all the affiliating churches. One example was the missionary program.

Based upon a unified budget, it collected funds for missions without informing the local church of which missionary it was helping. Some struggled with the idea of supporting liberal missionaries. Another example was the retirement and insurance program—often referred to as the "M and M Plan," or Ministers and Missionaries Benefit program—administered by the convention's Benefit Board. The retirement and insurance were completely lost to anyone who withdrew from fellowship with the convention. Some of the pastors and missionaries had paid premiums for many years, and if they left they lost the total financial investment. This made it extremely difficult for people to leave the convention. One further element that prohibited leaving was that the convention held mortgages on many church properties. If attempts were made not to conform to the leadership's demands, foreclosure was possible; if the church chose to withdraw its fellowship from the convention, the church property was retained by the convention.

Some of these convention controls were present in what has become known as the Wichita Case. When the convention met in Rochester, New York (June 1960), there were some objections to the convention's participation in the National Council of Churches. The delegates from the First Baptist Church of Wichita, Kansas, charging that the National Council was communistic and liberal, demanded that the convention withdraw its membership from the council. The General Council of the convention presented a resolution which reaffirmed the convention's continued participation in the National Council but which also stated that any local church had the right to "express dissent" or "withhold its financial support" of the National Council, and that such would be noted in the Yearbook. After debate, the convention delegates chose by a vote ratio of ten to one to continue participation in the National Council. Unhappy with the decision to cooperate with liberal Christianity, a majority of the eight hundred members of the First Baptist Church in Wichita voted constitutionally to withdraw fellowship from the American Baptist Convention and state and local associations. The 294 members voting in the minority filed for a court injunction to keep the property from passing into the hands of the majority. After two years of litigation, the

Kansas Supreme Court ruled in favor of the minority.[5] One Sunday, soon after the May 1962 court decision, the congregation voted to leave the property and the convention and, by prearrangement, the hundreds of the majority dramatically left the facility and began a new church in a large municipal hall. After the new church was fully operating and in its own facility, it voted to join fellowship with the Southern Baptist Convention.

During the litigation over the Wichita church, the General Council of the American Baptist Convention adopted a resolution addressed to the United States Congress (November 1961) deploring

> the release by congressmen, for general distribution, of unproved and unevaluated material secured from the House Committee on Un-American Activities. This material gives the false impression that certain of our outstanding American religious leaders are associated with communism. . . .
>
> We affirm our opposition to communism and protest guilt by association and the un-American practice of holding a man guilty until proven innocent.[6]

Ironically, the Social Creed of the National Council (Plank No. 2) advocated the "Social planning and control of the credit and monetary systems and the economic processes for the common good." And the same item quoted J. Edgar Hoover of the Federal Bureau of Investigation as saying, "The Communists are able to secure the ministers of the Gospel to promote their evil work and espouse a cause that is alien to the religion of Christ and Judaism."[7]

It appears that the Social Gospel influenced the American Baptist Convention to greater involvement in social problem solving than in gospel preaching, evangelism and missions. As involvement in urban center outreach, ecumenical union and later the desegregation movement increased, the number of missionaries decreased. The missionary force of the conven-

---

5. Torbet, *History of Baptists*, 461-462.
6. Ibid., 463.
7. American Council of Christian Churches, Literature Item No. 102.

tion had been eight hundred in 1923-1924 but by 1951 was only four hundred.[8]

Concerned with its weakening structure, the convention studied methods of reorganization during the 1960s. The results showed a deep concern for crucial social issues like nuclear war, racial tensions, religious intolerance, economic needs of under-developed nations and the spread of Communism.[9] To more effectively express and resolve their concerns, the American Baptist Convention reorganized along the lines of increased centralization of control, culminating in the 1972 decision to rename the convention the American Baptist Churches.

While liberalism seemed to snare many Northern Baptists, the more rural and conservative Southern Baptist Convention remained fundamental and evangelistic. Church memberships rapidly increased, missions expanded and its regional name lost some meaning as Southern Baptist churches appeared in each of the United States. However, liberalism did make some inroads in the South because of a conflict over a book by Dr. Ralph Elliott entitled, *The Message of Genesis*. Dr. Elliott, a professor at Midwestern Baptist Theological Seminary, advocated the rationalist position regarding criticism of the Scriptures, suggesting that there may have been more than one author for the book of Genesis, that Adam was not a real man but rather a symbolic term for all mankind, and that the flood of Genesis 6 was regional, not worldwide. To the historic, conservative Baptist this was heresy. The convention avoided a division by forming a special committee to ameliorate the situation. After a closer scrutiny of the seminaries revealed sympathy with Dr. Elliott's view, the convention became more willing to explore differing views of Biblical inspiration and interpretation.[10] Now, while the Southern Baptist Convention does not affiliate with the liberal National and World Councils of Churches, the denominational leadership has been favoring more and more liberal views.

8. Torbet, 464-467.
9. Ibid., 470.
10. Ibid., 475.

Some other Baptist groups chose to respond to the growing liberalism by joining with the National Association of Evangelicals, which emphasized their concern and opposition to the apostasy of liberalism but at the same time encouraged getting together for dialogue and better understanding of many viewpoints. The N.A.E. took a position of loving and caring for those with whom they disagreed rather than taking a militant stand. Their idea of piety was to enter into cooperative evangelistic enterprises such as "Key '73" or "I Found It," submerging theological differences in order to win souls.

While the liberal groups did not criticize the N.A.E. viewpoint, the fundamentalists, for the most part, did. However, the general Six-Principal Baptists, the Baptist General Conference and a New England Fellowship of Evangelical Baptists cooperated fully with the N.A.E., and even many pastors in separatist, fundamentalist churches shared their views and cooperated in various local situations. In reflection on the various theological divisions mentioned earlier in this chapter, we see a strong tendency toward new evangelicalism in this movement.

While the liberals and evangelicals practiced a loving cooperation and fellowship among the diverse religious factions, the fundamentalists tended toward continued separation. But even the fundamentalists were influenced by society, and theological separatism became legalism and then isolationism as the fundamentalists separated more and more from each other.

Dr. W. Wilbert Welch, president of Grand Rapids Baptist College and Seminary, prepared a handout in which the doctrine of separation was clearly set forth and verified through Scripture proof-texts. He concluded with some guidelines for implementing Biblical separation:

1. Distinguish carefully between the principle of separation and the practice of isolationism.
2. Distinguish carefully between Biblical separation and pharisaism. Pharisaism is rooted in spiritual arrogance, manifests a critical spirit, speaks with disdain and builds barriers over which few can climb.
3. Distinguish carefully between the spiritual unity of all

believers for which the Lord prayed and structural, organizational unity as promoted by ecumenists.

4. Endeavor to identify those various degrees of separation commonly spoken of as first, second, and third degrees in order to effect consistent judgment in both cooperation and association.

5. Avoid any practice or position made on the assumption that the end justifies the means employed. At no time should we condone what God condemns.

6. Exercise in every judgment a careful balance between truth and grace. Biblical separation is the careful discernment between truth and error—with the Word of God as the yardstick. Display as much grace as possible without compromising truth, and proclaim the truth not as a brutal club but as the Sword of the Spirit from a heart tendered by grace.

7. Ascertain facts about an alleged deviation from Biblical separation before pronouncing any personal or public judgment.

8. As far as possible, keep a door open for those brethren who may be struggling within a compromise situation and are sincerely seeking a Scriptural position and fellowship.

These guidelines reflect the position separatists have taken all through Baptist history. During the 1950-1980 era, some separatism tended to become either legalism or isolationism, or both. While many of the separatists maintained the historic attitude, many others turned on each other, fragmenting fundamental Baptist groups into many pieces of broken fellowship. Jealousies, power struggles, a form of "witch hunt," suspicion, judgmentalism, and other negative feelings and actions divided churches and created bitterness, which damaged the gospel witness. Most of these fragmentations did not come over important, Biblical conflicts but rather over petty human opinions and ideas.

It seems that secular humanism, preached against from many fundamentalist pulpits, had seeped into some church leadership and, with a verse of Scripture (not the Bible as a whole) to support it, had developed into a Christianized humanism. Instead of operating on the Baptist, congregational form of church government, powerful, manipulating pastors chose to operate as dictators. The little men with a great God had been lost in favor of great men doing exploits for God. Human criteria became the rule of determining whether God's blessing was upon a church. Faithfulness to the text of Scripture was sacrificed for promotional gimmickry, prayer became less important than programs, and spiritual sincerity was replaced by numbers and statistics. If a pastor was to be considered successful, his church had to have ever increasing numbers of *bodies* in attendance, be in the process of constructing a *building*, have an increasing financial *budget*, and for some years a *bus* ministry was an absolute requirement. Human boasting about these elements, and persistent slights against those who did not achieve them, began to divide brother from brother and church from church.

During the 1970s, another factor divided fundamentalist Baptists—the Christian school movement. Many local churches began Christian elementary and secondary schools in the church facilities to protect their youth from worldliness and at the same time indoctrinate them in the church's position. The potential for good was there, but if a church did not enter into such programs it was subtly made to feel less than successful. Thus the basis for fellowship was narrowed. The human spirit of competition and achievement strained legitimate Baptist relationships. Separation from apostasy had gotten out of focus, and separation based on extra-Biblical matters of hairstyle, clothing and personal practices became dominant.

It would be unfair to say that any of these factors were wrong in themselves, but they were becoming more important than the preaching of the whole Word of God, and evidence of God's blessing was being determined by human achievement. Thus Christian growth and development took on the appearance of humanism, even of Machiavellianism, which says, "might makes right," "the end justifies the means" and "man is the measure of all things."

Churches were begun by splitting off from other churches over power struggles and authority patterns. These churches then declared themselves to be "independent" Baptist churches and, playing upon special issues, many of them grew quickly in statistics. Ironically, there grew up many small associations of independent Baptist churches around the country.

An attempt to unify all fundamental Baptists around the world was made by the formation of the Fundamental Baptist Congress. It was to meet every three years for the enjoyment of fundamentalist preaching of Baptists from all over the world. It appears, however, that by the 1980s significant conflict over power and influence had decreased the effectiveness of the congress.

Modern Baptists are involved at almost every spot on the religious spectrum, from ecumenism to legalistic isolationism. While separation from apostasy is a Biblically provable doctrine, extreme fragmentation over less significant matters may seriously impede the future work in proclaiming the gospel of Christ and edifying believers. Only as the years pass will church historians be able to accurately evaluate the effects of fragmentation on the religious world.

11

Baptist Involvement
in Education

*The Baptists as a denomination have always attached little im-
portance to human learning as a qualification for the ministry,
in comparison with higher, though not miraculous, spiritual
gifts, which they believe it the province of the Holy Spirit to im-
part; and some of them, it must be acknowledged, have gone to
the extreme of looking upon high intellectual culture in a
minister as rather a hindrance than a help to the success of his
labors. But, if I mistake not, many . . . will show that the Baptists have had less credit as the friends and patrons of learning
than they have deserved.*

—Sprague

The educational practices of most societies in history have
involved dynamics of religious beliefs, social customs
and political philosophies. Each in its way added to the tensions, pulling the learning process one way or another. Ancient
educational systems sought a balance between utilitarian instruction and reliance upon the gods, whom they feared. The
classical world attempted to use education to put man in harmony with the natural forces of the world, including the gods.
The medieval world found education almost totally in the
hands of the Roman church, and instruction was primarily sectarian except for the practical instruction in warfare and also in

obedience to nobility and royalty. Renaissance education tried to mix the humanism of the classical world with the Christianity of the medieval world but gave man the prominent place. The Reformation was basically an attempt to modify deficiencies in the Roman church, and thus began the great conflicts between Protestantism and Catholicism, church and state and the Bible and natural observable forces. Since then, the war for the control of human minds has intensified.

The task of the modern educator is to balance intellectual discipline, social adjustment and Biblical truth. Proportional problems arise constantly between the religious and the secular in education. Ulich, of Harvard University, says:

> This conflict reflects the lack of balance between the polarities of freedom and authority, doubt and faith, speculation and empiricism. The problem cannot be understood without an insight into the great religious and philosophical components of our civilization.[1]

How important it is that the spiritual aspect be discovered and developed to counter the mechanistic world view.

Baptists have largely placed the emphasis on the spiritual or Biblical side of learning. The development of private education became a part of the great controversy over the separation of church and state. The Baptists joined other groups such as the Quakers, Dutch Reformed, German Lutherans and French Huguenots as "dissenters." Newman defines this form of dissent as "religious dissent—very strong religious dissent with an uncompromising and unrelenting spirit."[2] The Baptist contribution was quite different from the cultural rebellion of the 1960s.

> The early Baptists . . . were dissenters who had a firm grip on eternal things. Their dissent was meaningful because of this firm Biblical mooring. They did not advocate the immoral or an anarchy bred out of

1. Robert Ulich, *Philosophy of Education* (New York: American Book Company, 1961), 167.
2. Robert C. Newman, *Baptists and the American Tradition* (Des Plaines, IL: Regular Baptist Press, 1976), xi.

a cry for freedom without responsibility. We all owe
them a great debt.[3]

The Baptists entered the private, sectarian educational field
in 1756 when the Philadelphia Association established a Baptist school in Hopewell, New Jersey.[4] The Hopewell school was
one of the innovations in education—the academy. An
academy was often called "the private school in the city" or
"the advertised school" because it was an evening school in
the city offering special courses of instruction which were
advertized in the newspaper.[5] An academy had its control
vested in a board of trustees which may or may not have
operated under a state charter. The tuition costs were kept
moderate because the academic equipment was very small
and dedicated teachers were willing to accept lower salaries.
All academies, however, had to pay particular attention to
their individual support groups in curriculum development,
discipline and administration. Funds for the Hopewell school
were raised among Baptists in New Jersey and surrounding
states. Isaac Eaton, pastor of the Baptist Church in Hopewell,
was named as its first principal, and an old schoolhouse was
used for classes.[6] During the next one hundred years, sixty
Baptist academies were begun across the United States.

The success and popularity of the private school movement, including that of the Baptists, influenced public opinion. Butts quotes Illinois judge James Hall as saying in 1835:

If religious denominations think proper to educate
their children in their own tenets, they have a clear
right to do so. . . . In a country where religious opinions are unshackled, and men may believe and worship as they please, it seems to be unfair, that they
should not be allowed every facility for educating

3. Ibid., x.
4. R. Freeman Butts and Lawrence A. Cremin, A History of Education in
   American Culture (New York: Holt, Rinehart and Winston, 1953), 112.
5. H. G. Good, A History of Western Education (New York: Macmillan Company,
   1960), 388-389.
6. Richard B. Cook, The Story of the Baptists (Greenwood, SC: the Attic Press,
   1884), 372.

their children according to the dictates of their own judgement.[7]

As the private elementary and secondary schools proved successful, the Baptists established institutes in selected territorial areas to prepare ministers and missionaries. Some of these institutes were simply added-on courses to those of the academies, but some were begun separately. One example of a private Baptist institute was the Michigan and Huron Institute in Kalamazoo, Michigan, begun in 1833 by Thomas Merrill with financial assistance from the Baptist Convention of New York.[8] The purpose was to prepare men for service in churches and missions in the Michigan Territory. Later, in 1849, the Kalamazoo Theological Seminary began at the same location, and still later the entire school came under the direction of the Michigan Baptist Association and was renamed Kalamazoo College. While some Baptist institutes continued, most of them became either colleges or seminaries as the educational evolutionary process moved from institute to Bible college to Christian liberal arts college to liberal arts college.

The first Baptist college, Rhode Island College, was begun in Providence in 1764. As with many private colleges, someone had seen a need for a school with distinct purposes and exercised the proper technical and legal requirements to found one. Dr. James Manning had been a student at Hopewell Academy and went on to graduate from Princeton College with second honors in his class of 1762. This talented Baptist drafted a charter and was wise in avoiding some legislative pitfalls. The charter required that "the president, twenty-two trustees, and eight fellows were forever to be Baptists,"[9] but the other fourteen trustees were to represent the other denominational groups in Rhode Island. Dr. Manning served as president of Rhode Island College until his death in 1791, concurrently serving as pastor of the First Baptist Church in Providence. In 1804 the name of the school was changed to Brown

7. Butts, 223.
8. Torbet, *History of Baptists*, 315.
9. Vedder, *Short History*, 353.

University in honor of Nicholas Brown, who had given generously to its financial support.

A very famous court case regarding private education came before the United States Supreme Court in 1819. Although not a Baptist college, Dartmouth College was a private school. Political forces were moving to make state universities out of the colonial colleges. The state of New Hampshire had been providing money and land to Dartmouth, and some believed that the state should direct the use of this investment of public wealth. In 1815, New Hampshire sought, and legislation was passed, to secure control of Dartmouth on those grounds. The old board members, however, refused to accede to state demands, and for a while there were two Dartmouths. The old board appealed, but when denied they retained young Daniel Webster to appeal their case to the United States Supreme Court. The court accepted the case, and Chief Justice John Marshall wrote the decision declaring the legislation unconstitutional that would convert Dartmouth into a state university. The results were far-reaching. Private endowments and donations were guaranteed freedom from encroachment by the states, and contributions were fostered to private education already existing and to newly forming schools.[10]

Soon thereafter, some leaders began expressing the need for a deeper theological education in distinctively Baptist seminaries. It took several years to gain sufficient support, but in 1825 the Newton Theological Institution was founded in Newton Center, Massachusetts, under the direction of the Massachusetts Baptist Education Society. Professor Ira Chase, from Columbian University (presently George Washington University) in Washington, D.C., formed the new theological curriculum. Actually, he moved the whole theological department to Newton, bringing his students with him. While there had been other theological departments connected with Baptist colleges or universities, Newton Theological Institution was the first Baptist educational institution in America to be "devoted exclusively to a three-year theological curriculum for

10. Butts, 264-265.

college graduates.[11] Today, the school is known as Andover Newton Theological School.

Baptists, particularly in the South, were interested in providing schools with special programs for women. Alabama Baptists in the 1830s had organized three schools for girls, and other states were following their lead. In a typical nineteenth century statement, Cook commented:

> It is remarkable how many good schools we have for young ladies, especially in the South. Many young ladies in the North, bent upon obtaining an education, and yet contending feebly against the rigors of a northern winter, would find it to their profit to seek for what they want in these southern Baptist schools.[12]

The increasing emphasis on coeducational opportunities in the twentieth century has diminished the practicality and legality of segregated schools, whether based upon sexual or racial identities.

Since there were relatively few blacks in the North in the early twentieth century, the American Baptist Home Mission Society attempted to work with schools especially for blacks. At that time, blacks were not competitive with whites. The situation was different in the South, where Baptists cooperated with an interdenominational General Education Board to improve education for blacks. Together these efforts produced millions of dollars for education in academies, colleges and seminaries. By 1928, approximately 100,000 blacks had attended Baptist schools, and over 40 percent of them found their way into professional positions. Their education and enthusiasm over the years has been translated into thousands of churches with millions of church members across America. The actual result of the recent desegregation movement has yet to be evaluated objectively.

The nineteenth century saw Baptists establishing a long list of prominent colleges, universities and seminaries. Some are

11. Torbet, 311.
12. Cook, 377.

still closely identified with some arm of the Baptist movement, others only nominally so, still others not at all. A noncomprehensive list of these schools would include:

American Baptist Theological Seminary
Andover Newton Theological School
Baylor University
Bucknell University
University of Chicago
University of Chicago Divinity School
Colby College
Colgate Rochester Divinity School
Crozer Theological Seminary
Eastern Baptist College
Furman University
Hardin-Simmons University
Hillsdale College
Kalamazoo College
Southern Baptist Theological Seminary
William Jewell College

After the turn of the century, when Baptists came into serious conflict over theology (see chapter 9), many schools were established to reflect particular Baptist positions. The Northern Baptist Convention, for instance, began Northern Baptist Theological Seminary in Illinois in 1913 and Eastern Baptist Theological Seminary in Philadelphia in 1925.

While these schools tended to satisfy the conservative element within the convention, some fundamentalists were pointing to the emphasis of knowledge over faith and reason over Biblical absolutes in some older mainline schools. The liberals scorned the lack of education of some fundamentalists, calling them "funny-mentalists." Dr. R. T. Ketcham expressed colorfully in his preaching the fundamentalist view of well-educated liberals: "effervescent, soda water, fountain fizz, flat leaded, theological ninnyhammer-ites."

Ironically, the fundamentalists soon realized a need for an educated ministry based on the fundamentals of the faith and the separatist position. As a result, many such independent, fundamental Baptist colleges and seminaries were organized across the nation. Some of these fundamentalist schools are:

Baptist Bible College of Pennsylvania and
    School of Theology
Baptist Bible College and Seminary (Missouri)
Cedarville College
Central Conservative Baptist Seminary
Faith Baptist Bible College
Grand Rapids Baptist College and Seminary
Liberty Baptist College
Maranatha Baptist Bible College
Northwest Baptist Seminary
Pillsbury Baptist Bible College
Tennessee Temple Schools
Western Baptist College

Baptists have also managed to open a few institutes and seminaries outside the United States. Nearly every country in Europe has a Baptist seminary for national leaders, according to Rushbrooke. With the increase of affluency, many nationals have come to American schools to advance their education. While some have found this international experience a great benefit, others have found it difficult to make the adjustments related to returning home. A relatively new program is now being implemented in some far-reaching areas of the world—Theological Education by Extension. This program enables foreign nationals to be educated by means of correspondence and computers.

The push to establish traditional schools, and the rising Christian day school phenomenon, have presented new challenges among the Baptists. One of the greatest problems has been the balancing of operating costs with contributions and tuition. The numerous schools are forced to compete for funds, causing much innovative fund raising. To survive, each school seems to need an ever-increasing program of financial development, and the inflationary spiral of the past thirty years has forced numerous changes, compromises and in some cases bankruptcies.

Regardless of the frustrations and failures, Baptists have made a major mark in the educational world. While they may have fallen behind some of the other denominational programs of education, there is ample evidence that in preparing men and women of many racial, ethnic and national groups for the proclamation of the gospel, the Baptists have made valiant and noble contributions.

12

Baptists and Worldwide Missions

The missionary spirit of the Baptist denomination is its greatest strength, and its missionary record its greatest glory. Without boastfulness, and with no fear of being misunderstood or intelligently disputed, it may be said that Baptists, though perhaps having fewer missionaries and certainly contributing less money for Foreign Missions than several other great denominations in this country and Great Britain, are second to none in missionary success. . . . It is needed to instruct the young in our churches and the children in our Sunday Schools in the greatest work our denomination is doing, and to familiarize our people generally with the inspiring facts of our signally successful missionary history.

—A. H. Burlingham

Missions is commanded, encouraged and exemplified in the Bible. The idea of sending someone from a home base, supported by those of like faith, to people who have never heard the gospel, recurs over and over again in Scripture. The commandment given by the Lord to His disciples and to all believers in all ages is found in Matthew 28:19 and 20:

> Go ye therefore, and teach all nations, baptizing them in the name of the Father, and of the Son, and of the Holy Ghost: Teaching them to observe all

193

things whatsoever I have commanded you: and, lo, I
am with you alway, even unto the end of the world.
Amen.

Mark 16:15 records a similar command:

And he said unto them, Go ye into all the world, and
preach the gospel to every creature.

After His resurrection, Christ met with His disciples to remind them of the directives He had given them. There, just
prior to His ascension, the gathered followers perhaps remembered His statement recorded in John 20:21:

. . . as my Father hath sent me, even so send I you.

They may have felt very inadequate for that responsibility.
Jesus, Who had been their teacher, encourager and example
was about to leave them. How would they know what to do,
where to go, and how to share these great truths? Jesus had occasionally told them of another Comforter, of the same kind as
He, Who would come to aid them after He was gone away; but
in this traumatic moment that truth seemed almost blocked
from their minds. The patient Master read their faces and their
minds and made a startling statement, recorded in Acts 1:8:

But ye shall receive power, after that the Holy Ghost
is come upon you: and ye shall be witnesses unto
me both in Jerusalem and in all Judaea, and in Samaria, and unto the uttermost part of the earth.

And then they began to remember how Jesus had ministered in various towns around the area, and when He had
shared Himself and His teaching and His demonstrated power,
He would say to His disciples as in Mark 1:38:

. . . Let us go into the next towns, that I may preach
there also: for therefore came I forth.

Beginning in Acts 2, an account is given of the beginning of
missions, which would bring the message of saving grace
through faith in Christ to all who would receive the truth of the
Word and believe it with all their hearts. Peter, John, Stephen,
Philip, Paul, Barnabas, James, Silas, Mark, Lydia, Apollos,
Priscilla, Aquilla, Lois, Eunice, Timothy, Titus, and in turn their
various converts, reached out to forge link after link in the
chain of the family of God, stretching across the centuries until
this present moment in time.

After the historical record of the New Testament was completed, individuals who felt a special urging from God went with meager means to make Christ known to the people of heathen lands. Speaking of the Roman church of the medieval period, which did carry the gospel over much of the world, Hastings says:

> Mindful of the Last Will and Testament of Christ, the
> Church has always looked upon missionary work as
> an essential and solemn obligation, and upon its
> progress as an unfailing gauge of her vitality.[1]

In this spirit God's gospel was spread, even though, generally speaking, with an extreme amount of ritual and formalism.

With the apostatizing of the Roman church, and the confusion of the Protestant viewpoints, came the separatist movements and a renewal of enthusiasm for the spread of the gospel. World social and political conditions hampered much long-distance movement, but by the end of the eighteenth century the world was prepared by God for the advance of the gospel, and the great efforts in modern missions were begun.

The beginning of modern missions is generally attributed to William Carey. Carey was born near Northhampton, England, on August 17, 1761, the firstborn of a school teacher who instilled in him a mastery of language and desire for learning. Little escaped William's inquisitive mind—science, history, voyages, romances, Pilgrim's Progress. When he was fourteen years old, Carey became an apprentice to a shoemaker, which craft he followed with diligence. So precise and accurate was Carey's work that a pair of his shoes was kept on display as a model of good workmanship. Just when Carey became a Christian is hard to determine because different sources give different times, but the young shoemaker was a living demonstration of doing physical labor based on Christian principles.

On October 5, 1783, William Carey was baptized by Dr. Ryland and afterward was tutored in the faith by his pastor, Andrew Fuller.

About four years later, Carey was asked to preach, and he

1. Hastings, Encyclopedia of Religion and Ethics, vol. 8, 713.

said that he complied because he did not have sufficient confidence to refuse.[2] Carey had written about missions prior to
meeting Pastor Fuller but could not afford to have the material
printed. An unnamed deacon contributed the funds, and the
Christian world became richly challenged by *An Inquiry into the
Obligation of Christians to Use Means for the Conversion of the Heathens.*
In August 1787, Carey was ordained as pastor of the Baptist
Church at Moulton, England. His yearly salary was about
seventy-five dollars, which was only enough to feed his family
a few vegetables and no meat.

A memorable day came in May 1792, at the Baptist Association meeting in Nottingham. Carey preached a sermon based
on Isaiah 54:2 and 3:

> Enlarge the place of thy tent, and let them stretch
> forth the curtains of thine habitations: spare not,
> lengthen thy cords, and strengthen thy stakes;
>
> For thou shalt break forth on the right hand and on
> the left; and thy seed shall inherit the Gentiles, and
> make the desolate cities to be inhabited.

From his illumination of the text came his two famous ex-
hortations, "EXPECT GREAT THINGS FROM GOD; ATTEMPT
GREAT THINGS FOR GOD." Dr. Ryland evaluated the power
of the message:

> If all the people had lifted up their voice and wept,
> as the children of Israel did at Bochim (Judges 2), I
> would not have wondered at the effect; it would
> have only seemed proportionate to the cause; so
> clearly did he prove the criminality of our supine-
> ness in the cause of God.[3]

As a result of this powerful sermon, the Baptist Society for
the Propagation of the Gospel among the Heathens was begun
on October 2, 1792, at Kettering. From what had once been
hesitant and faltering lips came the inspiration launching the
great worldwide Baptist missionary enterprise. Subsequently,

---

2. G. Winfred Hervey, *The Story of Baptist Missions in Foreign Lands* (St. Louis:
Chancy R. Barns, 1885), 4.
3. Ibid., 5.

many other denominational and interdenominational societies and agencies were formed.

In 1793, Carey sailed for India as a missionary. His missionary efforts in India included evangelism, medical work, translation, printing and church establishing. Carey, Joshua Marshman, William Ward and John Thomas, M.D., worked together amid trial, persecution and death and saw marvelous answers to prayer. The message was always the same: attack the Hindu religion by preaching the gospel and teaching the commandments of Christ. Some had suggested that they should know all about Hinduism and teach the Hindu his error part by part. Carey's missionaries, however, have proven that:

> Whenever they preached the atonement of Jesus, and the love of the Father in giving His Son to die as our propitiatory sacrifice, the regenerating energies of the Holy Spirit have attended the message. Then the converts from the most venerable and most fascinating superstitions have exclaimed, "What have we any more to do with idols."[4]

William Carey died on June 9, 1834, and was buried beside his second wife. A simple epitaph inscribed beneath his name reads, "A wretched, poor and helpless worm, On Thy kind arms I fall." It is interesting to note that this man, who had contributed so much to missions, looked back over forty years of missionary work and exclaimed, "What hath *God* wrought!"

With this kind of stimulus, Baptists in America took up the work of sharing the gospel with every nation and people. In 1802, the Massachusetts Baptist Missionary Society was formed with this stated objective:

> To furnish occasional preaching and to promote a knowledge of evangelistic truth in the new settlements within these United States, or farther, if circumstances should render it proper.[5]

This society marks the beginning of the missions emphasis in America.

---

4. Ibid., 106-107.
5. Edward F. Merriam, A *History of American Baptist Missions* (Philadelphia: American Baptist Publication Society, 1900), 7.

In 1810, the American Board of Commissioners for Foreign Missions was formed because of the demands of some Andover Theological Seminary students. Under its direction, and with the approval of William Carey, nine people left America on a six-month journey to India. Among them were three who would play a major role in the shaping of American Baptist missions: Adoniram and Ann Judson aboard the ship *Caravan* and Luther Rice aboard the *Harmony*. Seminary studies had not clearly established the minds of these people regarding believer's immersion, but each individually became convinced by private study enroute, and each was subsequently immersed by William Ward in Calcutta. The Judsons and Rice resigned the American Board of Commissioners for Foreign Missions and wrote back to America encouraging the formation of a Baptist Missionary Society.

America was in a particularly favorable position to foster Baptist missions in the nineteenth century. The great wave of immigration from Europe brought many Baptists to America; the United States government was congenial toward the freedom for which Baptist principles called; and the Baptist ministry was adaptable to the wide variety of cultures and subcultures.[6]

Any new movement requires someone to act as the catalyst to bring the idea into reality. Dr. Thomas Baldwin, pastor of the Second Baptist Church of Boston, served to inspire American Baptist interest in missions. He and the Judsons had written each other about the need, and in 1813 Dr. Baldwin was instrumental in forming The Baptist Society for Propagating the Gospel in India and other Foreign Parts, assuming the support of the Judsons.

Luther Rice returned from India to serve as ambassador for foreign missions among the Baptist churches and associations in the United States. His ability to challenge and organize was instrumental in the starting of local and state missionary societies in New England and the Middle Atlantic states in 1813 and 1814.

In May 1814, Baptists from all over America met in Phil-

6. Cramp, *Baptist History*, 543.

adelphia to form a foreign missionary society representing all Baptists in America. The thirty-three delegates prepared and adopted a formal constitution, appointed the Judsons as the society's first missionaries and appointed Luther Rice to "continue his services in arousing the churches of this country to greater interest in the work of foreign missions."[7]

Baptist enthusiasm for missions was also evident in Germany. After Oncken's baptism, he established and strengthened Baptist churches among the German-speaking people in many European countries. Rushbrooke says it well regarding German missions in the nineteenth century:

> The Baptist movement is, indeed, one of the most remarkable features of the ecclesiastical history of the nineteenth century. In a time when the religious life of Germany was in bondage to rationalism and a rigid ecclesiasticism, the evangelical message was carried by laymen through the provinces. . . . there arose everywhere energetic Baptist churches, which carried on a mission rich in blessing for the non-churchly and non-Christian populace. . . . This was due to the fact that "every Baptist was a missionary."[8]

While American Baptist interest centered strongly on the Far East, some Baptists were looking toward Africa. The American Colonization Society had started a colony in Liberia, Africa, to which American slaves could go for freedom. The Negro Baptists in Virginia organized the African Baptist Missionary Society in 1814 for the express purpose of sending missionaries among these ex-slaves. For four years they tried to raise funds out of their poverty. In 1818, the Board of Managers of the General Baptist Missionary Society came to their aid, and in 1820 black missionaries Colin Teague and Lott Carey sailed for Africa. In 1824, Calvin Holton, a graduate of Waterville College, became the first white missionary to join the Negro missionaries in Liberia. During Holton's first year on

7. Merriam, 17.
8. Rushbrooke, *Baptist Movement*, 32.

the field he established a school and organized a local Baptist church.[9]

An interesting story of Negro missions is in the life of George Lisle, a slave who had been freed by his owner before the Revolutionary War for the purpose of preaching. Lisle became the first ordained Negro in the Baptist ministry, establishing the first Negro Baptist church near Savannah, Georgia, around 1778. When his former owner died Lisle feared reenslavement, so he borrowed funds to take him to Jamaica, where he preached extensively and formed a church in Kingston. His diligence was remarkable, for he repaid his loan by working as an indentured servant and saw five hundred converts baptized in eight years. While not receiving the publicity of Carey and Judson, Lisle became a missionary at least fifteen years before they did.

Baptists have tended to band together in a cooperative effort in missions more than in any other cause. The high cost of sending out missionaries has been more than one independent Baptist church can afford, making it necessary for several to work together. For this reason, numerous missionary societies and agencies have come into existence. Torbet lists the Baptist denominationally organized mission societies:

1792—Baptist Missionary Society (Britain)
1814—American Baptist Foreign Mission Societies
        (many associational societies, including
        black Baptists)
1842—Seventh Day Baptist Missionary Society
1845—Southern Baptist Convention, Foreign
        Mission Board
1861—Strict Baptist Mission (Britain)
1872—Scandinavian Independent Baptist Union
        (Sweden)
1873—Canadian Baptist Foreign Mission Board
1878—North American Baptist General Missionary
        Society
1880—National Baptist Convention, Foreign
        Mission Boards

9. Torbet, *History of Baptists*, 334.

1885—New Zealand Baptist Foreign Missionary
      Society
1889—Baptist Union of Sweden
1892—Oerebro Missionary Society (Sweden)
1897—Lott Carey Baptist Foreign Mission
      Convention
1913—Australian Baptist Missionary Society
1915—Norwegian Baptist Union Congo Mission
1923—Danish Baptist Mission
1923—Irish Baptist Foreign Mission
1933—Portuguese Baptist Convention
1935—Free Will Baptist Foreign Mission Board
1943—Conservative Baptist Foreign Mission
      Society
1944—Baptist General Conference, Board of
      Foreign Missions
1947—Missionary Commission of the Netherlands
      Baptist Union
1950—North American Baptist Association
1954—European Baptist Foreign Missionary
      Society
1959—Polish Evangelical Missionary Association[10]

During the modernist-fundamentalist conflict of the 1920s, many of these societies were infiltrated by modernists. As a result there developed a number of "independent, faith" Baptist mission agencies, with which the fundamental churches could identify. These agencies are not tied specifically to a Baptist denomination but serve many missionaries from various Baptist groups. The number of agencies fluctuates, but some of the better known ones include:

1921—Baptist Mid-Missions
1927—Association of Baptists for World
      Evangelism
1929—Evangelical Baptist Missions

All of the above mentioned boards, societies and agencies are primarily involved in foreign missions. To try to identify all

10. Ibid., 520-521.

the home mission societies is beyond the scope of this brief analysis.

Mission funds are gathered and distributed in two ways. The first is through a unified budget. Money is given to an agency budget, and the administrative board, not the contributor, decides which missionaries receive it. Although this method is relatively easy to administer, the contributor has no personal contact with the missionary and, conversely, the missionary has no accountability to the contributor. The second method requires the missionary to raise his own support from individuals and churches, and the mission agency simply acts as a clearing house for collection and distribution of funds. While this method is very cumbersome and difficult to administer, it does allow personal interaction between the contributor and the missionary.

The face of missions has changed radically in recent years. There once was a romantic attraction to missionary work, in the mystery of the "bush," the strange native costumes and the dramatic change in a native's life-style after conversion. But modern times have produced the ability to conveniently see and know about foreign lands, reducing the mystique. Urban growth and development in far-away countries has made the missionary's work very different from the days of a hut in a savage world, although some of that still remains.

So now we come to the heart of the whole matter. The mission of the church is not dependent upon our desire to have a better world, or to bring people of other cultures some of the benefits of our culture, or even the noble desire to share with them the best that we have in medicine, education, agriculture or science. The living, eternal heart of the church's mission lies in the mighty act of God in Christ, in which God takes the initiative to break down all barriers and cross over into the foreign lands of sin and death to make His love known. This is the mission movement, endless, forever in the act of God, and forever in the hearts and lives and work of men.[11]

11. Childers, *The Way Home*, 82.

> What manner of men ought they to be who have
> entered upon the great opportunities of the twen-
> tieth century, the inheritors of such a history? What
> boundless possibilities of growth, of achievement,
> lie before them! . . . How great will be their com-
> demnation if, having the wealth of opportunity in
> their hands, they squander it selfishly, or slothfully
> fail to make of the ten talents intrusted to them
> other ten that they may present with joy to their
> Lord at His coming![12]

The history of Baptist missions seems to be an endless expression of a single, overriding goal—reaching people for
Christ, whether through a hospital or school; through church
planting; through publishing or translation; through radio or
television presentations.

Should the Lord delay longer in His coming, others will
write of the exploits of missionaries of this and future centuries. In the words of one author:

> Even the future chronicler of their deeds in distant
> lands, as he lays down his pen of iron and rests his
> weary hand betimes, may he also renew his strength
> with the reflection that perhaps that poor worn-out
> pen is a sliver from the great sceptre of iron which
> the King of Kings holds in His right hand as He sits
> supreme upon His everlasting throne.[13]

12. Vedder, *Short History*, 382-383.
13. Hervey, 782.

13

Baptists and Evangelistic Movements

Great Harvester of bygone years
Thy fields prepare in rain of tears;
Or in the sunshine of the day,
Bring forth the ever-healing ray.

Great Harvester, Thou plowest deep
And breaking hearts do often weep.
Thy harrows o'er the soul doth go;
The soil to mellow here below.

The flood of trials and of grief
Break o'er the soul without relief,
Until the seeds of life arise,
Blending with blessings from the skies.

The lightnings flash, the thunders roll,
Souls seek for refuge in Thy control.
Blest safety find within Thy fold.
With tender mercy Thou dost hold.

Thy Word, the seed, doth slowly rise,
With sweetest joys to longing eyes.
To give the Gospel to Thy world,
Before Thy judgements soon are hurled.

And thus we yield our failing minds,
From all on earth that ever binds.
Great God, our Father, now we raise
Our voices in Thy endless praise!

                                                    —Joseph Larson

The churches of the New Testament settled into a pattern of evangelism very early in their development. The book of Acts describes the great success of the gospel as it expanded across the Roman world in spite of severe persecution. After the outpouring of the Holy Spirit, men of God moved to preach the gospel with power. Peter is the most prominent figure in the first ten chapters of Acts, sharing God's truths with large groups of Jewish people (Acts 2; 3), in the courts (Acts 4), in churches (Acts 5) and door to door (Acts 5). The chosen deacons help in evangelism (Acts 6—9), and then Peter is brought back to prominence with the revelation that God's gospel is to be taken to the Gentiles also (Acts 10). The rest of the book of Acts is a record of personal and public evangelism and church planting by Paul and those associated with him (Acts 9; 11—28).

Evangelism is basically a term used to describe the zealous preaching of the gospel, whether to large masses of people, to small groups, or in one-on-one personal contact. One purpose of this chapter is to examine trends in types of evangelistic outreach, but primarily the purpose is to look at the use of mass evangelism among the Baptists.

After the first century of the Church Age, mass evangelism does not seem to have prospered, if it was used at all. Local churches were active in preaching the gospel but, during medieval times, evangelism was nearly eclipsed by man's dependency upon the organized church rather than upon God. For a while, the gospel was being proclaimed only in isolated places, but by the year 1300 some itinerant preachers were speaking publicly to large groups of people in more populated areas. Men like Hus, Savonarola and Wycliffe spoke positively about the gospel of Christ while speaking out strongly against sin. Because the dominant church had become such a bureaucratic machine, these evangelists were persecuted and later martyred for the truth they proclaimed.

With the dawn of the Reformation came a new desire for in-depth knowledge of the Scriptures, and evangelism became a by-product of the scholarship of men like Luther and Calvin. So convinced were many leaders that they became very militant and forced people into conformity. Calvin, Zwingli and others waged actual military wars, Luther used the power of the pen with severity, Knox sought manipulative means to convert Britain to Christ, and Farel mastered the art of public preaching to win people to Christ. It is amazing to observe the abilities of these men as they worked tirelessly for God's truth. John Calvin, as an example, was a soldier, preacher, writer, philosopher and teacher all in one brief lifetime of fifty-five years.

The resolution of theological problems and the polarization of belief systems dominated the sixteenth and seventeenth centuries, as the major denominations were developed—Lutheran, Anglican, Presbyterian, Reformed, Methodist and Baptist. The conflicts between and among all of these, and the work of Roman Catholicism to redefine its position, kept mass evangelism from a significant place in religion.

The eighteenth century, however, saw a great new day dawn for evangelism. The preaching of men like George Whitefield, Jonathan Edwards, Gilbert and William Tennent and Theodore Frelinghuysen was typified by Edwards's famous sermon in 1741, "Sinners in the Hands of an Angry God." The emphasis of the preaching of the First Great Awakening was on the sinfulness of mankind, the salvation offered in Christ and the opportunity for all people to exercise their individual free wills in choosing to believe the gospel. The Baptists, both in Europe and America, were not generally supportive of this movement because they believed that it somehow violated the work of the local church. The First Great Awakening was short in duration due to the influx of rationalism and persecution.

In about 1795, however, the Second Great Awakening began, and this time the Baptists believed they should be involved. While the first movement had centered mainly in New England, the second found its strength in the Middle Colonies and then crossed over the Appalachians into the western frontiers. The greatest Baptist evangelistic progress was in Virginia, due to the work of two preachers, Shubal Stearns and Daniel Marshall.[1] The growth of Baptist churches between 1760 and 1790 was great as "pious ministers were stirred up to unusual exertion."[2] This growth may be properly called a "revival" because it awakened believers to the importance of reaching others.

> The ministers of those times were not satisfied with discharging the duties of their pastorates. They undertook long journeys, preaching as they went, often with no preconceived or definite plan, but travelling and labouring as they believed themselves to be directed from above. Mighty effects followed
> . . . the conversion of souls.[3]

There is something contagious in revivalism, as shown in someone's remark to a young preacher that if the preacher is on fire, people will come to see him burn.

The success of Baptists in evangelism on the frontier (such as in Kentucky and Tennessee, for example) was due basically to four factors:

1. The simplicity of Baptist doctrine
2. The democracy of Baptist organization
3. The ability to propagate the Baptist faith without overhead machinery
4. The Baptist appeal to the common man[4]

Probably no denominational body was better suited to deal with the restless, moving, changing frontier population than the Baptists. Seaboard Baptists moved over the mountains and settled there, working on farms, like the rest of the people, while preaching and starting churches. The Baptists had believed that the Anglican oppression in the Colonies was

---

1. Lars P. Qualben, A *History of the Christian Church* (New York: Thomas Nelson and Sons, 1973), 432.
2. Cramp, *Baptist History*, 512.
3. Ibid., 516.
4. William Warren Sweet, *Religion in the Development of American Culture* (New York: Charles Scribner's Sons, 1952), 110.

due to the fact that the Anglicans were too educated. This reaction was the beginning of a general Baptist prejudice against an educated and salaried ministry. Theodore Roosevelt spoke about the Baptist preachers who lived and worked exactly as their flocks, clearing ground, splitting rails, planting corn and raising hogs on equal terms with their parishioners.[5]

Out on the frontier, William Marshall (an uncle of Supreme Court Justice John Marshall) and Joseph and Isaac Redding were typical of the Baptist farmer-preacher approach. They preached with great zeal in their neighborhood. One young man, John Taylor, said that under their preaching, "the poor rags of my righteousness took fire and soon burned me to death."[6] Taylor later took his bride further into the frontier and founded a church. After harvesting his crops in the fall, he would travel as an itinerant preacher. Taylor thus serves as a prototype of the frontier Baptists involved in evangelism.

Revivalistic methods worked best on the frontier. Protracted meetings were characterized by long, exhortative, energetic preaching and enthusiastic singing. Services were held each night for two or three weeks and sometimes included afternoon or morning services as well. The main objective was to bring the simple gospel message to the great masses of religious illiterates. Here the appeal of the sermon was not so much to the intellect as to the heart and the conscience.

The Methodists soon joined the Baptists on the frontier and, either together or separately, employed the camp meeting method successfully. The use of music in these services created a need for hymnals. While many of the hymns appeared to be quite emotional and challenging, most of them were simple, "catch-on-to-quickly" songs with much repetition of phrases. Thus they served this particular culture well. While many songs taught Scriptural and doctrinal beliefs, some reflected a certain rivalry between the Methodists and Baptists. For example, the Methodists sang:

> We've searched the law of heaven,
> Throughout the Sacred code;

5. Ibid., 111-112.
6. Ibid., 112.

Of baptism there by dipping
We've never found a word.

To plunge is inconsistent
Compared with holy rites;
An instance of such business
We've never found as yet.

To this the Baptists responded with:
Not AT the River Jordan,
But IN the flowing stream
Stood John the Baptist preacher
When he baptized Him.

John was a Baptist preacher
When he baptized the Lamb;
Then Jesus was a Baptist
And thus the Baptists came.[7]

To be sure, this was a crude form of friendly competition, but it reflects the type of thing that stirred emotions and intellect in frontier evangelism.

By 1825, a simple concept of mass evangelism had been developed by men like Charles Finney—that of the professional evangelist. Others such as Reuben A. Torrey, J. Wilbur Chapman and Dwight L. Moody followed in this vein, using large halls and preaching to hundreds and thousands in the cities. Among the Baptists, the first professional evangelist was Jacob Knapp, in about 1830. Of Knapp it was said:

His statements of truth were devoid of all attempt at rhetorical finish, but he was unusually fervent and fluent. His mind was marked by strong logical tendencies and his sermons were full of homely illustrations, apt passages from the Bible, and close knowledge of human nature. In person he was short, squarely and stoutly built, his voice was sepulchral and his manner self-possessed; he was full of expedient and his will was indomitable. Crowds followed him, whole communities were moved by his labors and great numbers were added to the church.[8]

7. Ibid., 157-158.
8. Armitage, *History of Baptists*, 889.

Many such men desired to reach large numbers with the gospel, and by the late nineteenth century an evangelist-pastor was preaching weekly from nearly every pulpit.[9] Perhaps a classic example of this type of evangelist is Charles Haddon Spurgeon, who preached to thousands on a regular basis in London.

This new style of popular, mass evangelism employed preaching, singing, prolonged invitations, praying for the unconverted by name, encouraging women to speak and pray publicly and requiring sinners to come forward to the "anxious seat" for help in reaching a decision.[10] Although these tactics were sharply criticized, many adopted some version of them in evangelical churches.

In the post-World War I era, evangelism included opposition to social ills, especially in the form of temperance and prohibition movements. Billy Sunday was powerful and energetic in preaching the gospel, challenging the people to an interest in social problems and building Sunday Schools. He would usually lead a parade through city streets to the church where he was preaching, streams of people following after him. While many Baptist churches worked with Sunday and others, the movement of evangelism among Baptists was returning to an internal, every-member involvement in reaching others with the gospel.

In the twentieth century, evangelism has been expected to be a strong part of the fundamental Baptist ministry, each church expected to hold at least one protracted evangelistic meeting each year. Liberal Baptist churches have not participated much because of their liberal belief in the universal Fatherhood of God and brotherhood of man, which provides for all to enter Christ's kingdom. Liberalism also tends to emphasize the intellectual over the emotional in the Christian experience.

The barriers between Christian educators and evangelistic leaders are caused by different philosophical viewpoints of how to make the gospel message most effective. Criticisms of

9. Vedder, 351.
10. Torbet, 305.

evangelists by some educators include:

1. Emphasizing a momentary conversion decision without adequate application to life actions to make the decision significant

2. Asking for a verbal response to an appeal rather than a surrender to the will of God

3. Using techniques that reduce evangelism to supersalesmanship

4. More emphasis on quantitative results than qualitative life changes

5. Ignoring educational psychological principles of human growth, readiness and recognition of individual differences

6. Using terminology that is as superficial as that used in magic or to sell patent medicines

7. The symbolic language of evangelistic songs lacks realism in relating the gospel to everyday living situations

Evangelists, on the other hand, accuse the educators of the following:

1. Having an inadequate and limiting concept of God

2. Not accepting that all men by nature are equally lost

3. Having an inadequate conception of the Lordship and Saviorhood of Christ

4. Limiting the reality and power of the Holy Spirit

5. Having a limited view of the purpose and ministry of the local church

6. Having a romantic faith in educational techniques

7. Not recognizing the significance of life's crises and the importance of making immediate decisions

8. Lacking a sense of urgency regarding the need of lost men for salvation

9. Being so involved in problems of life that they lose the sense of ultimate meanings

As much interaction as there is in modern-day Christian work, it seems that Christian educators and evangelists could find some common ground of understanding. Among Baptists, however, these barriers continue to exist in one form or another, depending upon geographic and subcultural factors.

Moberg points out that "preoccupation with the ends of evangelism has blinded sincere religious leaders to implications of means they use."[11] The same may be said of the questionable methods of educators who attempt to reshape the thinking of students, whether in school or church settings.

There seems to be an endless amount of inventive techniques used in churches to promote both educational experiences and evangelism. For years churches relied upon the simple expression of Scriptural truths about man's sinfulness, God's provision of a Savior and the need to choose the way of God as the Holy Spirit produced conviction and response. In recent years, techniques have changed. They now vary from place to place and include revival-type mass meetings, colorful preaching, Bible comic books, recorded telephone messages, motion pictures, multi-media presentations, printed tracts, contests, quiz programs, gospel magic, spinning gospel tops and visitation evangelism. Technically, there is no limit to the methodology of evangelism and teaching and learning experiences, but it is imperative that great care be taken to keep the purpose and the glory of God in proper perspective. Vigilance must be maintained to assure that:

1. Promotional techniques are not deceptively propagandist.
2. Proof texts are not distorted by removing them from the context.
3. Quotations, misquotations, and unfair comparisons are properly credited.
4. Reality is maintained at all times.
5. Both the means and the end are justified.
6. Psychological trickery is not employed.
7. Advertisements and other means of church outreach are used with the highest level of Christian ethics possible.
8. Conversions are followed up by careful instruction in the Scriptures.

There have been a few influential ecumenical evangelistic

---

11. David O. Moberg, *The Church as a Social Institution* (Englewood Cliffs, NJ: Prentice-Hall, Inc., 1962), 211.

movements in operation since the days of the modernist-fundamentalist conflict. However, the predominant evangelistic force, at least among Baptists, has been the local church employing many techniques in outreach, including the professional evangelist. Many pastors who are strongly evangelistic serve other churches in campaigns to reach people for Christ. The great dilemma facing Christianity, and strongly challenging Baptists, is that conversions are not keeping up with the world's population growth. Is it possible that Biblical salvation programs, working ineffectively in the hearts, minds and lives of people, is what Jesus meant in His parable of the "unjust judge"? After giving the illustration, He asked this penetrating question:

Nevertheless when the Son of man cometh, shall he find faith on the earth? (Luke 18:8).

14

Baptist Participation in Social Action

Lord, let me live from day to day
    In such a self-forgetful way;
That even when I kneel to pray
    My prayers will be for others.

Help me in all the work I do,
    To ever be sincere and true;
And know that all I do for You
    Must needs be done for others.

Let self be crucified and slain,
    And buried deep, and all in vain
May efforts be to rise again
    Unless to live for others.

And when my work on earth is done;
    And my new work in heaven begun;
May I forget the crown I've worn
    While thinking still of others.

Others Lord, yes others,
    Let this my motto be;
Help me to live for others
    That I may live like Thee.

—Anonymous

It is difficult when thinking of Baptist activity in social concerns to separate it from political involvement. While there are always the laws of the land to consider with regard to social problems, there is a compelling sense that it is the Christian's responsibility to be concerned for those "less fortunate." Nearly all Baptist churches have a benevolent fund or deacon's fund which is administered separately from the church budget to assist people in times of economic difficulty. The scope of human social needs, however, goes much beyond that kind of effort.

A scanning of the first five books of the New Testament reveals that Christ and His apostles helped the hungry, the physically handicapped, the emotionally distraught and the grieving. In each case, however, they assisted these people to open the way for the greater concern—the spiritual well-being of the individual(s). Paul wrote to Timothy about meeting social needs, particularly of widows, and James sounds a similar note in his epistle. It is evident that Scripture teaches the responsibility of Christians to aid those who are in need, regardless of whether they are in the church fellowship.

Many large denominations with episcopal or presbyterian types of church government, which have a hierarchy of church directiveness, have been involved in social work denominationally. The Baptists, however, with their emphasis on local church sovereignty and democratic government, do not have the denominational machinery to make a coordinated effort in meeting social needs.

Individual Baptists within the local churches generally have differing viewpoints on social issues. Even though a Biblical stand is declared, positions are taken based on economic conditions, social background and political allegiance as well as religious convictions. Although Baptists have always been primarily "common people" and have rarely been in positions of community leadership, they have made many indirect contributions. Areas of involvement in social problems before the middle of the twentieth century would include:

1. Full manhood suffrage in England
2. Abolition of slave trade in England
3. Influence in the American slavery issue

4. Reducing child labor abuses in factories
5. Improving working conditions for women in industry
6. Aiding in prison reforms
7. Working for general literacy
8. Passive resistance to laws harmful to family and morals
9. Emphasizing religious liberty—especially from state encroachments
10. Caring for aged ministers and missionaries
11. Working for more satisfactory interracial relationships
12. Seeking alternative methods for settling international disputes other than by war
13. Feeding and clothing needy people regardless of culture or nationality
14. Encouraging participation in chaplaincies
15. Working with temperance and prohibition movements

Since 1950, Baptists have become more specifically involved in:

1. The needs of people whose countries were ravaged by war
2. Alcohol and drug rehabilitation programs
3. The civil rights movements
4. The human rights movements—especially abortion
5. Children's programs for those from broken homes, unwed mothers, delinquents, adoptions, foster placements and day-care centers
6. Family struggles and dysfunctions
7. Personal counseling programs
8. Retirement and aging problems

It is essential to understand that Baptists serve in these matters in a very unstructured way. They encourage individual participation through preaching and teaching. Rarely, if ever, have Baptists moved en masse to bring relief to social problems. Reviewing discussions and policy statements of several major Baptist denominations reveals that any direct work is mostly with hospitals, children's homes and homes for the aged.

Loren Ames, of the Woodland Association of Southern Baptists, shared in a telephone conversation with the author that the Southern Baptist Convention technically owns and operates only one social institution—a children's home in New Orleans. All other Baptist children's homes, retirement homes and hospitals in the South are owned and operated either by local associations or privately, and are "approved" by the convention as worthy of their support. The 1983 Annual of the Southern Baptist Convention does not even list the agencies that are "approved" except for the seminaries.

The American Baptist Churches declare that they hold to local church sovereignty and institutional autonomy. According to Robert Shaw of the Michigan office of the denomination, the Board of the American Baptist Churches "approves" numerous institutions for funding, cooperation and service, but the relationship between the denomination and each institution is strictly voluntary.

The Baptist General Conference "formally endorses" three children's homes and six retirement homes nationally, but they are independently operated. While the local churches may feel free to cooperate with and support financially these institutions, there is no structural requirement.

Among separatist Baptist movements, the General Association of Regular Baptist Churches will serve as an example. They approve two children's agencies, one child placement agency, one retirement home and one agency for the mentally retarded. Each is privately operated.

One observation about Baptist social institutions is that each seems closely tied to some local association, particularly in the formative years. As it grows, it tends to become more independent and grows away from the denomination. Some even separate completely from the denomination, either because they have taken on some characteristics of which the denomination disapproves or because they no longer need the support. It seems that those which separate have a strong tendency to turn to government funding and become more secular in approach.

W. R. Wagoner, a Baptist children's home superintendent in North Carolina, says:

> Many of the children we serve have been let down,
> disappointed by adults, and they have lost their faith
> in grown-ups. They have lost their faith in them-

selves. They have lost faith in God. We take every child as he comes to us and we try to rebuild in him the faith that he has lost, letting him know that somebody cares for him, that there is love and affection to be shared with him. No matter what has gone before he can square his shoulders, look the world in the face, be grateful for being alive and for being himself. He can take advantage of all the opportunities around him and have confidence about what lies ahead. He has the right to work and the privilege of worship, and no other man has more.[1]

T. Sloane Guy, of the Southern Baptist Hospital Board, commented on the function of the wellness center in the ministry of Baptists:

A Baptist hospital is established, of course, to care for the physical needs of men and women and to provide compassion; but we should all understand that it is here primarily because of the nature of God and the example of Jesus. The teaching of the Gospel is that God is concerned with whatever happens to people; Jesus himself showed this concern and sympathy whenever He encountered human need. The care of the sick is a part of the Christian mission, a part of evangelism; and we will therefore go on opening hospitals and caring for the sick. We will also see that these hospitals are more than merely places of medicine and surgery; we will do our best to maintain them as Christian institutions where a man can find an answer to his spiritual longings as well as his physical needs.[2]

Gerald Gingrich, of the American Baptist Churches, wrote of the large numbers of aged people and the need to incorporate social care with spiritual underpinnings:

This is a major segment of our population, and we are all becoming aware of these people among us and they have special needs. . . . The government is

1. Childers, *The Way Home*, 117.
2. Ibid., 127.

taking this into account with its amazing development of health and welfare activities, and there is a
whole new philosophy concerning the aged. They
are now to be reckoned with economically, socially,
politically. Never before in the history of mankind
have so many people lived so many years. Never
before have churches had such an opportunity for
expanding their ministry for older people.[3]

For Baptist churches to see social areas as opportunities
for ministry, they will have to recognize the institutions as ex-
tensions of the work of the local church. When this idea is accepted as true, the work will not be thought of as a Social
Gospel, but as a means of meeting the needs of others and of
drawing them to the Savior.

3. Ibid., 136.

15

Baptist Practices in Political Affairs

. . . It is important to remember that Baptists did not isolate themselves from the state, as many European Anabaptists did. Baptists were among the most loyal soldiers and supporters of the American Revolution, and Baptists were one important pressure group which insisted that the First Amendment, the first item of the Bill of Rights, be part of the Constitution.

. . . The state cannot tell the churches what to preach or tell individuals what to believe; and the church, in turn, cannot ask for state money or official influence to support religious activities. Congress and the judiciary have protected the religious liberties guaranteed in the First Amendment. . . .

There is nothing about being a Christian and a Baptist which prevents one from being a loyal citizen, and there is nothing about being a citizen which prevents one from being a Baptist. Separation of church and state does not prevent church property from being tax free, and all the armed services have chaplains paid with government money. Many churches feel there is nothing inconsistent about having an American flag on one side of the sanctuary and a Christian flag on the other, or urging their members to vote on election day. More important, many Baptists feel that our religious convictions compel us to be concerned for the state.

—Harold Stassen

If we are to discuss Baptist involvement in political issues, we must go back to the very beginning of the Baptist movement, in seventeenth century England. True, Christians of all ages had experienced some form of persecution, with little recourse. But by and large, true Christians had been Separatists rather than actively attempting to change existing political and social structures. The seventeenth century English Baptists carried this example further as they laid the foundation for future Baptist positions: When all reasonable and peaceful attempts failed, physical separation was carried out.

This principle was used when King James I, of England, said of the threatening "sectaries," "I will make them conform, or I will harry them out of the land."[1] This was the last possible position, and the Baptists and other Separatists fled to Amsterdam for safety.

Upon the changing of men on the royal throne, the Baptists returned to England to establish churches in their homeland. A statement in the Baptist Confession of 1644 concerned the relationship between churches and government:

> XLVIII. A civil magistracy is an ordinance of God, set up by him for the punishment of evil-doers, and for the praise of them that do well; and that in all lawful things, commanded by them, subjection ought to be given by us in the Lord, not only for the wrath, but for conscience' sake; and that we are to make supplications and prayers for kings, and all that are in authority, that under them we may live a quiet and peaceable life in all godliness and honesty.
>
> The supreme magistracy of this kingdom we acknowledge to be King and Parliament . . . and concerning the worship of God, there is but one lawgiver . . . which is Jesus Christ. . . . So it is the magistrate's duty to tender the liberty of men's consciences, . . . and to protect all under them from all wrong, injury and molestation . . . And as we cannot do anything contrary to our understandings and consciences, so neither can we forbear the doing of

1. Vedder, *Short History*, 202.

that which our understandings and consciences bind us to do. And if the magistrates should require us to do otherwise, we are to yield our persons in a passive way to their power, as the saints of old have done.[2]

This statement was Landmarkism at its best. It marked the first written statement of religious liberty, advocating the right of all men to worship God, each according to the dictates of his own conscience, without hindrance from any earthly power (government). While considered revolutionary in 1644, this pioneer statement would be subscribed to by most Christian groups nearly 300 years later.

From time to time, Baptists were accused of sedition and other serious crimes, but generally without justification. In 1665, however, the infamous Five-Mile Act was passed in England. Nonconformist ministers (including Baptists) were prohibited from living within five miles of any city or borough, or from passing closer than within five miles of any established church except on a "high road." A fine of forty pounds (a considerable amount) was to be imposed on all violators. Another law, the Conventicle Act, made it illegal for more than five persons to gather for worship in any place other than an established church which used the liturgy. Violators received severe penalties of fines, imprisonment and exile.

In those times many of the Baptists were lionhearted men, good soldiers of Jesus Christ, obeying God rather than man, and remembering the divine injunction, "forsake not the assembling of yourselves together." Though the vilest of laws were in full operation, and the country swarmed with spies who were hired by the bishops, they courageously met for the worship of God by scores and hundreds, in private houses, or in woods, or at midnight; and what is still more worthy of admiration, they founded churches which have been preserved and prospered. . . . Some of these heroic defenders of faith were sent to prison for a breach of the laws named

2. Ibid., 212.

above, but from their dungeons they wrote in the following strain: "Our societies from which we are taken are exceedingly cheerful, and a very lively spirit of faith and prayer is amongst them, and their meetings rather increase than otherwise. Sure that the Lord is near, his wondrous works declare; for the singing of the birds is come, and the voice of the turtle is heard in the land."[3]

Benedict further quotes Sir James McIntosh: "The Baptists suffered more than any other under Charles II, because they publicly professed the principles of religious liberty."[4]

For many years after these events, the English Baptists were able to influence both the construction and enforcement of legislation. In writings, in preaching and in personal living, they carried significant weight in the land as they championed the cause of religious liberty.

The nineteenth century, with its emphasis on social reform, gives us little information about Baptist involvement in political action, except for their continuous insistence upon honesty, decency and human dignity in dealing with social ills. Baptist participation in the antislavery movement came the closest to political involvement in America, but they were divided along sectional lines—proslavery in the South and generally abolitionist in the North.

In America, the struggle for a free religious climate in cooperation with a free government actually began with the Baptists. Before John Locke began to write his philosophy advocating personal, religious and political freedoms, Roger Williams was exerting influence for a free church in a free state.

For the subsequent history of what became the United States, Roger Williams possesses one indubitable importance, that he stands at the beginning of it. Just as some great experience in the youth of a person is ever afterward a determinant of his personality, so the American character has inevi-

3. David Benedict, A *General History of the Baptist Denomination in America* (New York: Lewis Colby and Company, 1853), 324.
4. Ibid.

tably been molded by the fact that in the first years of colonization there arose this prophet of religious liberty. Later generations may not have always understood his thought; they may have imagined that his premises were something other than the actual ones, but they could not forget him or deny him. He exerted little or no direct influence on theorists of the Revolution and the Constitution, who drew on quite different intellectual sources, yet as a figure and a reputation he was always there to remind Americans that no other conclusion than absolute religious freedom was feasible in this society. The image of him in conflict with the righteous founders of New England could not be obliterated; all later righteous men would be tormented by it until they learned to accept his basic thesis, that virtue gives them no right to impose on others their own definitions. As a symbol, Williams has become an integral element in the meaning of American democracy along with Jefferson and Lincoln.[5]

With these liberties framed into the First Amendment and the Bill of Rights of the American Constitution, the Baptists have been dedicated to encouraging their maintenance. As the years have passed, more and more control of social problems has been given to legislative and executive functions of government. Since 1950, the judicial branch has become involved in the interpretation of the laws to such an extent that morality is now based on sociological law, or on human reason and a practical, present expedient.

Many Baptists have joined other religious groups to press for legislation on moral questions of abortion, education, taxation and family protection. Organizations such as the Moral Majority have been developed to lobby *against* causes they believe have a humanistic base or violate Christian liberty and *for* causes they believe have substantial Biblical bases.

In this very involved world, it is difficult to maintain the

5. Green, *Roger Williams and the Massachusetts Magistrates*, 110.

careful separation between church and state. The North Carolina Baptist Convention recognized the problem in 1959 and set forth the following six basic principles:

1. Each has distinct reasons for being, so church and state have different basic functions.
2. Each has separate publics, the government including all persons born in its territory and the church including only those who are part of the fellowship of faith.
3. Each has different methods, the state using police power, military action, and taxation to achieve its objectives and the church using instruction, worship, prayer and love rather than compulsion.
4. Each has separate administrations, with neither using the other to achieve its own ends.
5. Each has separate sources of support, so churches depend on stewardship and not on tax funds for revenue.
6. Each has separate educational programs, so neither will monopolize channels of knowledge.[6]

It appears, however, that the church and state in America have become so intertwined that separation serves as nothing more than a guide to action on both sides. Nowadays each influences the other in numerous ways.

Government influences churches in their relationship to the rest of society:

1. By state regulations regarding incorporation
2. By state regulations on property ownership
3. By state and local rules regarding zoning
4. By state and local enforcement of safety regulations
5. By state control of construction (barrier-free and designated numbers of parking spaces for the seating capacity)
6. By state requirements of financial reporting for tax exemption purposes and employee tax withholding
7. By state intervention in cases of religious practices that

6. Moberg, *Church as Social Institution*, 371-372.

tend to injure the health, safety and morals of the public

8. By state sanctioning and licensing of Christian educational operations
9. By state protection and assistance by counsel and legal means of missionaries to foreign lands
10. By state support of chaplains in Congress, the Armed Forces and correctional institutions
11. By the state giving numerous indirect economic benefits to churches, religious institutions and Christian workers

On the other hand, churches exert certain influences on government, some direct, some indirect.

1. By direct efforts to effect changes in political affairs by letters, resolutions, petitions, etc.
2. By providing sanctions for civil or human rights movements by appealing to Biblical injunctions, ethics and adherence to traditional customs of society
3. By teaching Biblical, moral absolutes in support of the American way of life
4. By employing the principles of religious liberty for all, churches have influenced government in immigration policies, relationship with Israel and acceptance and/or rejection of atheistic Communism
5. By pressuring government to promote specific values by legislation against liquor, gambling, pornography, discrimination, political corruption and nuclear war
6. By pressuring government to pass legislation favorable to the family, child welfare, education and other social and economic issues
7. By encouraging election of believers to public office

The sovereignty of the local church among Baptists makes a common voice in politics extremely difficult. Nevertheless, Baptists have found ways to function at grass roots levels to put pressure on the political process.

Because of the increasing centralization of government, with its extensive power of the courts, many Baptists feel that the careful balance between church and state is teetering in favor of government. Invasions of religious privacy are being met with various degrees of compliance and opposition. It can only be hoped that the problems between church and state over spheres of dominance can be resolved without deeper violations of freedom for either party.

The Baptist movement has an exceptional history of contributions to the political processes, especially in America. Its principles of freedom have a sharp focus in the present world. They will have an impact tomorrow. Much of the relationship between Baptists, in particular, and the state was, is, and hopefully shall continue to be one of involvement in the lives of all humanity as worthwhile and dignified creatures in the "image of God."

Bibliography

Armitage, Thomas. A *History of the Baptists*. New York: Bryan, Taylor and Company, 1890.

This old material is an excellent, detailed story of the Baptists. While he spends a lot of time on the very beginning of church history, he still covers with objectivity the Baptist story to 1890. The book has been reprinted in a two-volume set by Maranatha Baptist Bible College.

Asman, Lorence. *The Tragic Fall of the First Baptist Church*. Grand Rapids: Asman Tract Publishers, 1956.

This is a brief account of the Fountain Street Baptist Church in Grand Rapids, Michigan, which became one of the most liberal churches in America.

Benedict, David. A *General History of the Baptist Denomination in America*. New York: Lewis Colby and Company, 1853.

The material is highly documented and quotes many people of Baptist antiquity. It does not follow a chronological order but deals more by subject.

Butts, R. Freeman, and Lawrence A. Cremin. A *History of Education in American Culture*. New York: Holt, Rinehart and Winston, 1953.

Secular writers discuss the history of education in general.

Carrol, J. M. *The Trail of Blood*. Lexington: Clarence Walker, 1931.

A very widely read booklet demonstrating the position that there has been an endless chain of people of Baptist persuasion from John the Baptist onward.

Cathcart, William. *The Baptist Encyclopedia*. Philadelphia: Louis H. Everts, 1883.

Although no longer in print, this book is a treasure of Baptist information.

Childers, James S., ed. *The Way Home*. New York: Holt, Rinehart and Winston, 1964.

This is a collection of articles about Baptists and their contributions to society.

Cook, Richard B. *The Story of the Baptists*. Greenwood, SC: the Attic Press, Inc., 1884. Reprinted, 1973.

This is a very difficult book to get into but does have some valuable details and insights about Baptists.

Cramp, J. M. *Baptist History*. London: Elliot Stock, 1868.

This is a well-documented history in readable style.

Fulton, Howard C. *What Regular Old-fashioned Baptists Stand For*. Rochester, NY: Interstate Evangelistic Association, Inc., 1935.

Essentially this is a copy of a sermon on Baptist distinctives delivered at the annual meeting of the General Association of Regular Baptist Churches.

Good, H. G. A *History of Western Education*. New York: Macmillan Company, 1960.

This general history of education begins with the earliest records of education and works through to the functioning of American education.

Greene, Theodore P., ed. *Roger Williams and the Massachusetts Magistrates*. Boston: D.C. Heath and Company, 1964.

These are mainly transcripts of the participants of the Colonial conflict between Williams, Cotton and others, with some analyses by historians.

Hastings, James. *Encyclopedia of Religion and Ethics*. 12 vols. New York: Charles Scribner's Sons, 1922.

A wide-ranging general religious encyclopedia.

Hervey, G. Winfred. *The Story of Baptist Missions in Foreign Lands*. St. Louis: Chancy R. Barns, 1885.

A very fine, detailed explanation of the purpose and application of Baptist missions.

Hiscox, Edward T. *The New Directory for Baptist Churches*. Philadelphia: Judson Press, 1953.

This book is the standard manual for operating Baptist churches.

Hull, Merle R. *What a Fellowship! The First Fifty Years of the General Association of Regular Baptist Churches*. Schaumburg, IL: Regular Baptist Press, 1981.

Ketcham, Robert T. *Facts for Baptists to Face*. Rochester, NY: Interstate Evangelistic Association, 1936.

This booklet provides quotations regarding the growth of modernism among the Baptists.

Krieger, Leonard. *Kings and Philosophers, 1689-1789*. New York: W. W. Norton and Company, 1970.

A general secular history text on the period.

Lumpkin, William L. *Baptist Confessions of Faith*. Valley Forge, PA: Judson Press, 1969.

A collection of the various confessions of faith authored by Baptists through the centuries.

Mead, Frank S. *Handbook of Denominations in the United States*. Nashville: Parthenon Press, 1980.

This document is edited annually listing each denomination with a brief statement of history and statistical data.

Merriam, Edward F. *A History of American Baptist Missions*. Philadelphia: American Baptist Publication Society, 1900.

A very interesting book detailing the story of Baptist missions in America to 1900.

Moberg, David O. *The Church as a Social Institution*. Engelwood Cliffs, NJ: Prentice-Hall, Inc., 1962.

A general sociology of religion text written by a Baptist sociology professor.

Newman, Robert C. *Baptists and the American Tradition*. Des Plaines, IL: Regular Baptist Press, 1976.

This book briefly discusses Baptist participation in dissent in the Colonies.

Orchard, G. H. *A Concise History of Baptists*. Texarkana, TX: Bogard Press, 1977 (originally published in 1855).

This author's position is that Baptists began in the New Testament.

Qualben, Lars P. *A History of the Christian Church*. New York: Thomas Nelson and Sons, 1973.

A general church history textbook.

Reese, J. Irving. *A Guide for Organizing and Conducting a Baptist Church*. Hayward, CA: J. F. May Press, 1952.

This book gives in simplified terms the appropriate polity and procedure in starting new Baptist churches.

Rushbrooke, J. H. *The Baptist Movement in the Continent of Europe.* London: The Kingsgate Press, 1923.

Here is a country-by-country history of the Baptists as they began on the Continent.

Schaeffer, Francis. *How Should We Then Live?* Old Tappan, NJ: Fleming H. Revell Company, 1976.

A fascinating analysis of the modern culture in Christianity.

Stowell, Joseph M. *The General Association of Regular Baptist Churches: Background and History.* Hayward, CA: J. F. May Press, 1949.

The only presently available history of this denomination.

Sweet, William Warren. *Religion in the Development of American Culture.* New York: Charles Scribner's Sons, 1952.

A general history of religion on the American frontier.

Torbet, Robert G. A *History of the Baptists.* Valley Forge, PA: Judson Press, 1969.

This is a textbook on the history of Baptists up to the end of the 1950s. Very detailed; not easy reading.

Ulich, Robert. *Philosophy of Education.* New York: American Book Company, 1961.

The title gives the basic idea of the book: it is a history of educational philosophy.

Vedder, Henry C. A *Short History of the Baptists.* Philadelphia: the American Baptist Publication Society, 1907.

This is good material, written while the author was still in agreement with evangelical Baptist beliefs.

Wallbank, T. Walter, and others. *Civilization Past and Present*. Glenview, IL: Scott, Foresman and Company, 1971.

One of the better records of the secular history of civilization with some perceptive comments.

Weniger, G. Archer. *Ecumenical Folly*. Wheaton, IL: Sword of the Lord Foundation, 1961.

An exposé of the liberalism in the National Council of Churches.

Editorial. "Is Evangelical Theology Changing?" *Christian Life*, (March 1956).

Hart, Rollin. November 1925. *Forum*.

Ketcham, Robert T. "The Princeton Case." *Baptist Bulletin* (May 1940).

Moulds, G. H. "The Conflict between the Modernists and the Fundamentalists in the Northern Baptist Convention since 1920." *Baptist Bulletin* (January 1941).

Must Freedom Perish? Literature Item No. 102. New York: American Council of Christian Churches.

June 1962. *The Baptist World*.

Reprint from the April 1954 issue of the *Crusader* upon resolution of the General Council of the American Baptist Convention.

Subject Index

Act of Toleration, 95
Act of Uniformity, 108
Albigenses, 41-42. *See also*
  Waldenses
American Baptist Association
  (Landmarkism), 64-65, 82
American Baptist Churches in
  the USA, 65, 68, 83, 174-177,
  218-219. *See also* Northern
  Baptist Convention
American Council of Christian
  Churches, 168-169
Anabaptist Kinship Theory,
  42-43
Anabaptists, 39, 42-43, 77, 80,
  91, 106, 134
Anglican church. *See* Church of
  England
Apostles' Creed, 73, 76
Apostolic Church Successionist
  Theory, 38-39, 42
Apostolic Era, 22
Apostolic Fathers, 21-22
Arminianism, 57, 60, 91

Associations and conventions,
  difference between, 55

Baptism, believer's, 39-40, 42,
  44, 58, 92-93, 98, 100, 106,
  129-130, 132. *See also* Immersion; Infant baptism; Pouring;
  Sprinkling
Baptist Bible Fellowship, 69, 70,
  157
Baptist Bible Union, 68, 83,
  153-154
Baptist Distinctives, 24, 37,
  40-42
Baptist General Conference,
  63-64, 178, 218
Baptist Missionary Association,
  69
Baptist origins within the
  Roman Catholic church,
  theory of, 44-47
Baptist Union, 59, 98-99
Baptist World Alliance, 71, 100,
  127, 135

235

Scripture Index